COLOUR MEASUREMENT AND MIXTURE

LECTOR HOUSE PUBLIC DOMAIN WORKS

COLOUR MEASUREMENT AND MIXTURE

WILLIAM DE WIVELESLIE ABNEY

ISBN: 978-93-89701-76-0

Published: 1891

LECTOR HOUSE LLP
E-MAIL: lectorpublishing@gmail.com

Colour-Patch Apparatus.

THE ROMANCE OF SCIENCE.

COLOUR MEASUREMENT AND MIXTURE.

BY

CAPTAIN W. DE W. ABNEY,
C.B., R.E., D.C.L., F.R.S.

PUBLISHED UNDER THE DIRECTION OF THE COMMITTEE
OF GENERAL LITERATURE AND EDUCATION APPOINTED BY THE
SOCIETY FOR PROMOTING CHRISTIAN KNOWLEDGE.

WITH NUMEROUS ILLUSTRATIONS.

1891.

PREFACE.

Some ten years ago there were three measurements of the spectrum which I set myself to carry out; the last two, at all events, involving new methods of experimenting. The three measurements were: (1st) The heating effect; (2nd) the luminosity; and (3rd) the chemical effect on various salts, of the different rays of the spectrum. The task is now completed, and it was in carrying out the second part of it that General Festing, who joined me in the research, and myself were led into a wider study of colour than at first intended, as the apparatus we devised enabled us to carry out experiments which, whilst difficult under ordinary circumstances, became easy to make. On two occasions, at the invitation of the Society of Arts, I have delivered a short course of lectures on the subject of Colour, and naturally I chose to treat it from the point of view of our own methods of experimenting; and these lectures, expanded and modified, form the basis of the present volume.

As a treatise it must necessarily be incomplete, as it scarcely touches on the history of the subject—a part which must always be of deep interest. The solely physiological aspect of colour has also been scarcely dealt with; that part which the physicist can submit to measurement being that which alone was practicable under the circumstances.

W. DE W. ABNEY.

South Kensington,
1st May, 1891.

CONTENTS

Chapter   *Page*

Preface. vi

I. Sources of Light—Reflected Light—Reflection from Roughened Surfaces—Colour Constants. 1

II. A Standard Light—Formation of the Spectrum by Prisms and by the Diffraction Grating—Wave-lengths of the principal Fraunhofer Line—Position of Colours in the Spectrum. 4

III. The Visible and Invisible Parts of the Spectrum—Methods for showing the Existence of the Invisible Portions—Phosphorescence—Photography of the Dark Rays—Thermo-Electric Currents.. . . .11

IV. Description of Colour Patch Apparatus—Rotating Sectors—Method of making a Scale for the Spectrum. 16

V. Absorption of the Spectrum—Analysis of Colour—Vibrations of Rays—Absorption by Pigments—Phosphorescence—Interference. . . .21

VI. Scattered Light—Sunset Colours—Law of the Scattering by Fine Particles—Sunset Clouds—Luminosities of Sunlight at different Altitudes of the Sun.. 26

VII. Luminosity of the Spectrum to Normal-eyed and Colour-blind Persons—Method of determining the Luminosity of Pigments—Addition of one Luminosity to another. 32

VIII. Methods of Measuring the Intensity of the Different Colours of the Spectrum, reflected from Pigmented Surfaces—Templates for the Spectrum.. 39

IX. Colour Mixtures—Yellow Spot in the Eye—Comparison of Different Lights—Simple Colours by mixing Simple Colours—Yellow and Blue form White. 57

X. Extinction of Colour by White Light—Extinction of White Light by Colour. 64

XI. Primary Colours—Molecular Swings—Colour Sensations—Sensations absent in the Colour-blind. 68

XII. Formation of Colour Equations—Kœnig's Curves—Maxwell's Apparatus and Curves. 74

XIII. Match of Compound Colours with Simple Colours—All Colours reduced to Numbers—Method of matching a Colour with a Spectrum Colour and White Light. 79

XIV. Complementary Colours—Complementary Pigment Colours—Measurement of Complementary Colours. 84

XV. Persistence of Images on the Retina—The Use of Coloured Discs.. 90

XVI. Contrast Colours—Measurement of Contrast Colours—Fatigue of the Eye—After-Images. 99

Index. 103

LIST OF ILLUSTRATIONS

Fig.		Page
	Colour-Patch Apparatus.	iv
1.	Spectrum of Sunlight.	4
2.	The Carbon Poles of an Electric Light.	5
3.	Curve for converting the Prismatic Spectrum into Wave-lengths.	9
4.	The Thermopile.	13
5.	Heating effect of different Sources of Radiation.	14
6.	Colour Patch Apparatus.	17
7.	Rotating Sectors.	18
8.	Spectrum of Sodium Lithium and Carbon.	19
9.	Interference Bands.	24
10.	Absorption of Rays by the Atmosphere.	29
11.	Luminosity Curve of the Spectrum of the Positive Pole of the Electric Light.	33
12.	Rectangles of White and Vermilion.	35
13.	Arrangement for measuring the Luminosities of Pigments.	35
14.	Measurement of the Intensity of Rays reflected from white and coloured surfaces.	39
15.	Intensity of Rays reflected from Vermilion, Emerald Green, and French Ultramarine.	41
16.	Method of obtaining two Patches of identical Colour.	44
17.	Absorption by Red, Blue, and Green Glasses.	46
18.	Light reflected from Metallic Surfaces.	47

19. 1. Vermilion 2. Carmine. 3. Mercuric Iodide. 4. Indian Red. 48

20. 1. Gamboge. 2. Indian Yellow. 3. Cadmium Yellow. 4. Yellow Ochre. . . 49

21. 1. Emerald Green. 2. Chromous Oxide. 3. Terre Verte. 50

22. 1. Indigo. 2. Antwerp Blue. 3. Cobalt. 4. French Ultramarine. 51

23. Method of obtaining a Colour Template. 51

24. Template of Carmine. 52

25. Template of Luminosity of White Light. 53

26. Absorption of transmitted and reflected Light by Prussian Blue
    and Carmine. 54

27. Collimator for comparing the intensity of two sources of Light. 54

28. Spectrum Intensities of Sunlight, Gaslight, and Blue Sky. 55

29. Comparison of Sun and Sky Lights. 56

30. Slide with slits to be used in the Spectrum. 57

31. Screen on which to match Gamboge. 59

32. Diaphragm in front of Prism. 65

33. Curve of Sensitiveness of Silver Bromo-iodide. 69

34. Curves of Colour Sensations. 70

35. Kœnig's Curves of Colour Sensations. 76

36. Maxwell's Colour-box. 76

37. Maxwell's Curves of Colour Sensations. 78

38. Chromatic Circle. 85

39. Disc to cause alternate opening and closing of two Slits. 90

40. Disc painted Blue and Red. 91

41. Electro-motor with Discs attached. 92

42. Method of cutting Disc to allow an overlap of a second Disc. 92

43. Arrangement to find value of Gamboge in terms of Emerald Green
    and Vermilion. 95

44. Disc arranged to give approximately all the Spectrum Colours. 97

45. Method of showing Contrast Colours. 99

COLOUR MEASUREMENT AND MIXTURE.

CHAPTER I.

Sources of Light—Reflected Light—Reflection from Roughened Surfaces—Colour Constants.

There is nothing, perhaps, in our everyday life which appeals more to the mind than colour, yet so accustomed are the generality of mankind to its influence that but few stop to inquire the "why and wherefore" of its existence, or its cause. To those few, however, there is a source of endless and boundless enjoyment in its study; for in the realms of physical and physiological science there is perhaps no other subject in which experiments give results so fascinating and often so beautiful. Although its serious study must be undertaken with a clear mind, a good eye, and a fair supply of patience, yet a general idea of the subject may be grasped by those who are possessed of but ordinary intelligence.

Colour phenomena are encountered nearly every day of one's life, and the fact that they are so frequently met with, prevents that attention to them, or even their remark. Who amongst us, for instance, has noticed the existence of what are called positive and negative after images, after looking at some strongly illuminated object, or would have gauged the fact that a certain portion of the nervous system can be fatigued by a colour, and give rise to images of its complementary, had not an enterprising advertiser, who manufactures a household necessary, drawn attention to it in a manner that could not be misunderstood.

If on an autumn afternoon we pass through a garden whilst it is still perfectly light, we can notice the gorgeous colouring of the flowers, and appreciate with the eyes the beauty of each tint. As evening comes on the tints darken, the darkest-coloured flowers begin to lose their colour, and only the brightest strike the eye. When night still further closes in every colour goes, though the outlines of the flowers may still be distinguished; and it would not be impossible, in some parts, to see a tiny speck of pale light upon the ground amongst them. This speck of light we should know from experience to be the light from a glow-worm. Why is it that we lose the colour of the flowers and recognize the tiny light from this small worm? The reason for the one is that in order for objects which are not self-luminous to be seen at all, light must fall on them and illuminate them, and the light which they reflect may be coloured if they possess the qualities to reflect coloured light. The glow-worm's light is seen, not because it does not emit light in the day-time, but because the eye, being limited in sensitiveness, is unable to distinguish it when it is flooded with the light of day. The glow-worm, however, is self-luminous, as is shown by the fact that it emits light in the dark, the light itself being slightly coloured if compared with that of day. That a candle-flame or the sun is self-luminous is an axiom, and need not be philosophised upon; but what must be impressed on the reader is, that though an object which requires to be illuminated to be seen, is not self-luminous, yet when illuminated it does in fact become a source of illumination to the eye, although the light is only light reflected from its surface. It is a point worth remembering that the rougher the surface of an object, the brighter to the eye it will be. That is, a coloured object when polished will be a bad secondary source of illumination, as the light incident upon it will be very nearly reflected from the surface, according to the ordinary laws of reflection; but if it be roughened it will become a much better source, as the roughnesses, though obeying the laws of reflection, will reflect light in every direction. A good example of this is an ordinary sheet of glass. Light from a source falling on its surface is scarcely reflected in any direction except in that determined by the ordinary laws of reflection, and it will be scarcely visible to the eye. Grind its surface, however, and the innumerable facets caused by the grinding will reflect light back to the eye in whatever position it be placed, and will thus be distinctly seen.

We may here premise that even the roughest surface will reflect a greater percentage—varying greatly according to the nature of the surface—of light in the direction which it would do if it were a smooth surface than in any other; and in taking measurements of the light irregularly reflected from a rough surface, this fact must be borne in mind.

Not only must we know how colour is produced, but we must also be able to refer it to some standard which shall be readily reproduced, and which shall be unalterable. There are two variable factors which have to be taken into account in colour experiments: the first is the quality of light which illuminates the object, and the second is the sensitiveness of the eye which perceives it, as light is only a sensation which is recognized by the brain through the medium of the eye. We shall, as we go on, see that different qualities of light may cause objects to appear of different hues, and further that eyes may vary in perceptive power, to an extent of which the large majority of people are not aware. Hence it becomes necessary as far as possible to eliminate these variables.

The task which we have set ourselves to perform then, is first to find a suitable light for experimental work, and next to endeavour to refer colour to an eye which has no abnormal defects. This being accomplished, we have then to find means to measure the different constants which are involved in colour, and to refer the measurements to some standard. Colour constants are three, viz. hue, luminosity, and purity; and it will be seen that if these three are determined, the measurement of the colour is complete.

Perhaps the meaning of these terms may require to be explained. The hue of a colour is what in common parlance is often called the colour. Thus we talk of rose, violet, magenta, emerald green, and so on, but for measuring purposes the hue had best be referred to the spectrum colours as a standard (the means of doing so will be shortly explained), for they are simple colours, which can be expressed by numbers. Compound colours, which it may be said are invariably to be found in nature, being mixtures of simple colours, can be just as readily referred to the spectrum. By the luminosity of a colour we mean its brightness, the standard of reference being the brightness of a white surface when illuminated by the same white light. By the purity of a colour we mean its freedom from admixture with white light. An example of different degrees of purity will be found in washes of water-colours of different tenuity. Thus if we wash a sheet of paper with a light tint of carmine, the whiteness of the paper is not obliterated; if we pass another wash over it the whiteness of the paper is lessened, and so on. The lightest tint is that which is most lacking in purity.

CHAPTER II.

A Standard Light—Formation of the Spectrum by Prisms and by the
Diffraction Grating—Wave-lengths of the principal Fraunhofer
Line—Position of Colours in the Spectrum.

As we have to turn to the spectrum for pure and simple colours, from which
we may produce any compound colour we may wish to deal with, we will first
consider the light with which we shall form it. A spectrum may be produced from
any source of light, such as sunlight, limelight, the electric light, gaslight, or incandescence electric light, as also from incandescent vapours, or gases; but it is only a
solid which is, or is rendered incandescent, that will give us a *continuous* spectrum,
as it is called, that is, a spectrum which is unbroken by gaps of non-luminosity, or
sudden change of brightness, throughout its length.

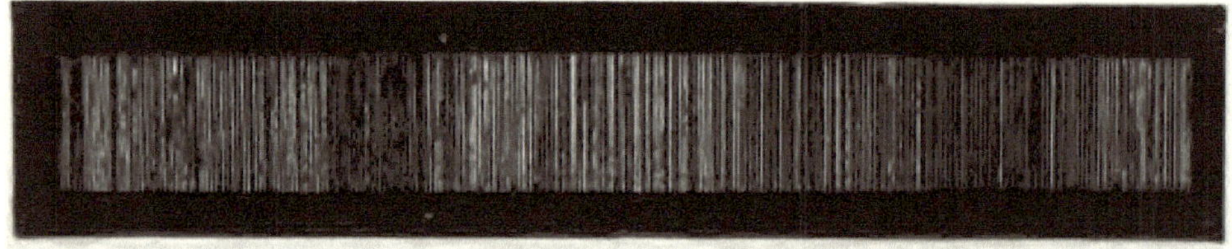

FIG. 1.
Spectrum of Sunlight.

The great desideratum for the study of colour is a light which not only gives
a practically continuous spectrum, but one which is produced by the radiation
of matter which is black when cold, and which can be kept at a constantly high
temperature. We have purposely said "black" in the sentence above, since it is be-
lieved that differently coloured bodies, when heated to equal temperatures, might
not give the same relative intensities to the different parts of the spectrum, the
variation being dependent on the colour of the heated body. A black body must
always give the same visible spectrum when heated to the same temperature. The
spectrum of sunlight (Fig. 1) is not continuous, as we find it crossed by an innumerable number of fine lines of varying breadth and blackness. This want of conti-
nuity would not be fatal to its adoption were it possible to use it outside the limits
of our atmosphere, as then, unless the temperature of the sun itself changed, the
spectrum produced would be invariable; but unfortunately the relative brightness
or luminosity of the different parts of the spectrum varies from day to day, and
hour to hour, according to the height of the sun above the horizon (see Chap. VI.);

and its integral brightness varies according to the clearness of the sky. It is evident then, that, as a reference light, sunlight is most unsuitable, so we may dismiss it from our possible standards.

FIG. 2.
The Carbon Poles of an Electric Light.

By the process of elimination we may arrive at the light upon which we can rely, for the purpose we have in view, viz. the production of a spectrum of moderate size, and sufficiently bright to be well viewed when projected upon a screen. For some purposes, as for instance in becoming acquainted with the general character of the spectrum, a feebler light, such as gaslight, or light from electrical glow lamps, may be employed, since the spectrum may be viewed directly by the eye without the intervention of a screen. They have two drawbacks for our object: one being the want of general intensity, and the other the feeble luminosity of blue and violet rays in their spectrum (see page 110). The limelight we can also dismiss for want of steadiness. Its whiteness and luminosity varies according to the oxygen playing on the lime cylinder, rendering the relative intensities of the different parts of the spectrum so erratic as to make it unreliable. This leaves the (electric) arc-light as the only one which is really available. Remember how the arc-light is produced. A current of electricity passes between the ends of two thick black carbon rods, or poles as they are called, through an air space of small interval, and the passage of the current renders the tips of these rods white-hot (Fig. 2). The centre of the end of one pole, called the positive pole, where a crater-like depression is formed, is the part which attains the whitest heat, and its temperature seems to be constant, and to be that of the volatilization of carbon. Numerous experiments have been made by the writer, and he has found that the light emitted by this crater in the positive pole is, within the limits of the error of observation, always of the same whiteness, and consequently gives a spectrum which is unvarying in the proportionate intensities of the different colours. When the experiments made to determine the luminosity of the spectrum are described, the method of ascertaining this will be readily understood.

In the spectrum produced by this light there are two places in the violet where there are bands of violet lines slightly brighter than the general spectrum. They are principally due to the light emitted from the incandescent vapour of carbon, which is volatilized and plays between the two poles (see Fig. 2); but as these bands are of but small visual intensity, and situated towards the limit of the visible spectrum, they do not interfere with eye-measures of colours, though they do, to a certain extent, to the analysis of radiation by photography. If we throw the positive pole a little behind the negative pole we can, however, considerably mitigate this evil. We can separate the carbon rods to such a degree that the white-hot crater faces the observer, and a good deal of the arc is hidden. This is well seen in the figure.

We have now described the light we have adopted, and the reasons for adopting it; and having obtained our light, we can now consider by what plan we shall form our spectrum. There are two ways open to us — one by glass prisms, and the other by a diffraction grating. Glass prisms separate white light, or indeed any light, into its components, from the fact that the refraction of each coloured ray differs from every other. Thus the red rays are least refracted, and the violet the most, and the yellow, green and blue are intermediate between them, being placed in the order of least refrangibility. Between these there is of course every shade of simple colour, one melting into the other. In order to form a pure and bright spectrum with prisms, in a room of limited dimensions, we have to use certain auxiliary apparatus which are not positively essential, though convenient. The real essentials to form a spectrum are a narrow slit, a glass prism, with perfectly plane faces, and a lens. If this be the only apparatus available, the slit must be placed at a long distance from the prism, the beam of light must pass through the slit on to the prism, and the lens must be placed at such a distance from the slit that it forms a sharp image on a screen. When the light passes through the prism, the screen will have to be rotated in the arc of a circle, so that its distance from the slit measured along the line of the ray to the prism, and from the prism to the screen, is the same as it would be without the intervening prism. An apparatus of this description is not convenient, however, as it requires much more space than is often available. If a lens be placed between the slit and the prism, at exactly its focal length from the former, the light entering the slit will, after passage through the lens, emerge as parallel rays, that is, they will emerge as they would do if the slit were placed at an infinite distance from the observer.

The focal length of this collimating lens need not be greater than twelve to eighteen inches, so that the great space required by the cruder apparatus is very much curtailed. The lens and slit are mounted one at each end of a tube of the necessary length, and are thus handy to use.

Instead of one prism two or three may be used, giving an angular dispersion of the spectrum two or three times respectively greater than that which would be given by only one prism; consequently to obtain a given length of spectrum with the increased dispersion, the focal length of the lens used to focus the image on the screen may be diminished.

The drawback to the use of prisms is that the dispersion of the red end of the spectrum is much less than that of the blue end, and is apt to give a false impression as to the relative luminosities of, and length of spectrum occupied by, the different colours. In some text-books it is told us that the diffraction grating gives us a dispersion which is in exact relation to the wave-length. This is not true, however, as it can only give one small portion in such relationship, and that only when it is specially set for the purpose. The subject of diffraction is one into which it would be foreign to our purpose to wander. We may say that for measures such as we shall make, it is handier to employ prisms, as the prismatic spectrum is more intense than the diffraction spectrum. This can be readily understood when we consider the subject even superficially. If we throw a beam of light on a grating which contains perhaps some 14,000 parallel lines in the space of one inch in width, the lines being ruled on a plane and bright metallic surface, and receive the reflected beam on a screen, the appearance that is presented is a white central spot, together with six or seven spectra of gradually diminishing brightness on each side of it, all except the first pair overlapping one another. That these different spectra do exist can be readily shown by placing in the beam a piece of red glass, when symmetrical pairs of the red part of the spectrum will be found, one of each pair being on opposite sides of what will now be the central red spot. Half the light falling on the grating is concentrated in this central spot, and the remaining half goes to form the spectra; the pair nearest the central spot being the brightest. We thus are drawn to the conclusion that at the outside we can only have less than one-quarter of the incident light to form the brightest spectrum we can use. With two good prisms we use at last three-fourths of the incident light, so that for the same length of spectrum we can get at least three times the average brightness that we should get were we to employ a diffraction grating.

We must now refresh the reader's memory with a few simple facts about light, in order that our meaning may be clear when we speak of rays of different wave-lengths. Every colour in the spectrum has a different wave-length, and it is owing to this difference in wave-length that we are able to separate them by refraction, or diffraction, and to isolate them. Light, or indeed any radiation, is caused by a rhythmic oscillation of the impalpable medium which we, for want of a better term, call ether, and the distance between two of these waves which are in the same phase is called the wave-length of the particular radiation. The extent of the oscillation is called the amplitude, which when squared is in effect a measure of the *intensity* of the radiation. Thus at sea the distance between the crests of two waves is the wave-length, and the height from trough to crest the amplitude; and the intensity, or power of doing work, of two waves of the same wave-lengths but of different heights, is as the square of their heights. Thus, if the height of one were one unit, and of the other two units, the latter could do four times more work than the former. The waves of radiation which give the sensation of colour in the spectrum vary in length, not perhaps to the extent that might be imagined, considering the great difference that is perceived by the eye, but still they are markedly different. The fact that the spectrum of sunlight is not continuous, but is broken up by innumerable fine lines, has already been alluded to. The position of these lines is always the same, as regards the colour in which they are situated, and is absolutely fixed directly we know their wave-length; hence if we know the wave-lengths of these lines, we can refer the colour in which they lie to them. Now some lines of the solar-spectrum are blacker and consequently more marked than others, and instead of referring the colours to the finer lines, we can refer them to the distance they are from one or more of these darker lines, where these latter are absolutely fixed; in fact they act as mile-stones on a road.

In the red we have three lines in the solar spectrum, which for sake of easy reference are called A, B and C; in the orange we have a line called D, in the green a line called E, in the blue F, in the violet G, and in the extreme violet H. These lines are our fiducial lines, and all colours can be referred to them. The following are the wave-lengths of these lines, on the scale of **1/10,000,000** of a millimetre as a unit

A	7594
B	6867
C	6562
D	5892
E	5269
F	4861
G	4307
H	3968

When the spectrum is produced by prisms the intervals between these lines are not proportional to the wave-lengths, and consequently if we measure the distance of a ray in the spectrum from two of these lines, we have to resort to calculation, or to a graphically drawn curve, to ascertain its wave-length. For the purpose of experiments in colour the graphic curve from which the wave-length can immediately be read off is sufficient. The following diagram (Fig. 3) shows how this can be done.

The names and range of the principal colours which are seen in the spectrum has been a matter of some controversy. Professor Rood has, however, made observations which may be accepted as correct with a moderately bright spectrum. If the spectrum be divided into 1000 parts between A in the red, and H, the limit of the violet, he makes the following table of colours.

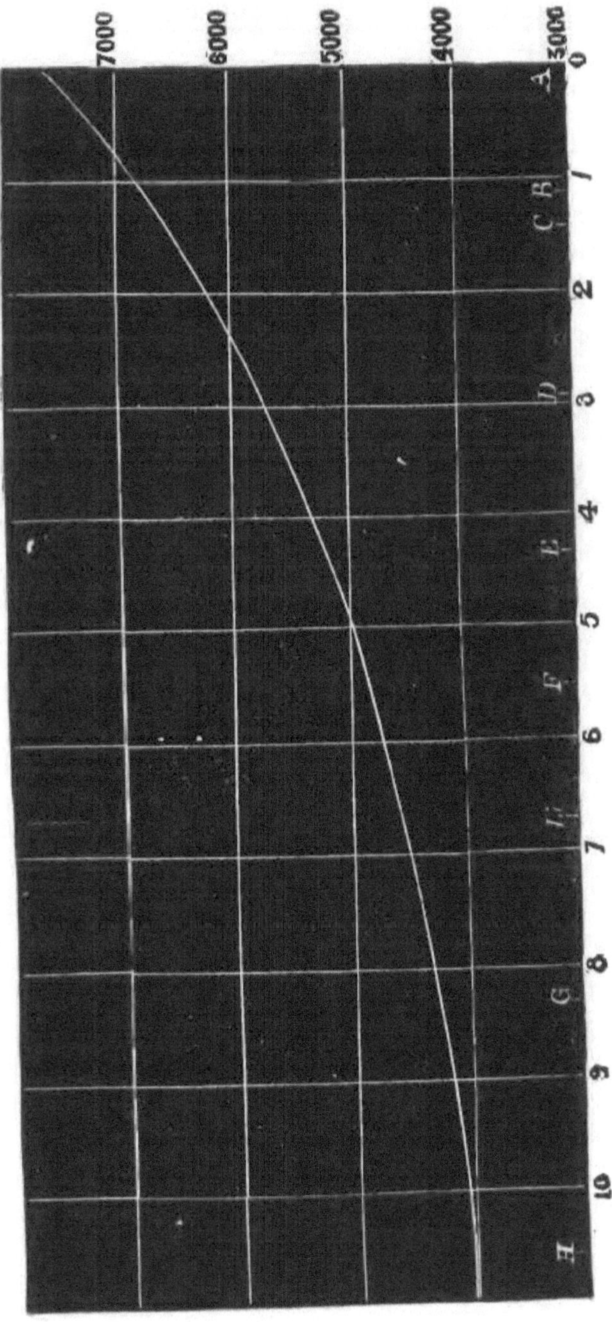

FIG. 3.
Curve for converting the Prismatic Spectrum into Wave-lengths.

Scale.	Colour.
0 to 149	Red.
149 to 194	Orange red.
194 to 210	Orange.
210 to 230	Orange yellow.
230 to 240	Yellow.
240 to 344	Yellow green and green yellow.
344 to 447	Green and blue green.
447 to 495	Azure blue.
495 to 806	Blue and blue violet.
806 to 1000	Violet.

In the above scale (Fig. 3) A = 0, B = 74·0, C = 112·7, D = 220·3, E = 363·1, F = 493·2, G = 753·6, H = 1000.

These are the main subdivisions of colour, but it must be recollected that one melts into the other. When the spectrum is very bright the colours tend to alter in hue; thus the orange becomes paler, and the yellow whiter, and the blue paler. On the other hand, if the spectrum be diminished in brightness the tendency is for the colours to change in the opposite direction. Thus the yellow almost disappears and becomes of a green hue, whilst the orange becomes redder, and the spectrum itself becomes shorter to the eye than before.

Let us strictly guard ourselves, however, from the criticism that all eyes see not alike. Suffice it to say that the above table is correct for the ordinary or normal eye, and does not necessarily apply to those who have defective vision as regards colour sensation.

CHAPTER III.

The Visible and Invisible Parts of the Spectrum—Methods for showing the Existence of the Invisible Portions—Phosphorescence—
Photography of the Dark Rays—Thermo-Electric Currents.

We are apt to forget, when looking at the spectrum, that what the eye sees is not all that is to be found in the prismatic analysis of light. The spectrum, it must be recollected, is not limited to those rays which the eye perceives. There are rays both beyond the extreme violet and below the extreme red, which exist and which exercise a marked effect on the world's economy. Thus, rays beyond the violet are those which with the violet and the blue rays principally affect vegetation, enabling certain chemical changes to take place which are necessary for its growth and health; whilst the rays below the red are those possessing the greatest amount of energy, and if they fall upon bodies which absorb them, as very nearly all bodies do to a certain extent, they heat them. The warmth we feel from sunlight is principally due to the dark rays which lie below the red of the spectrum.

The existence of both kinds of these dark rays may be demonstrated in a very simple manner by the effect that they produce on certain bodies. For instance, there is a yellow dye with which cheap ribbon is dyed, which if placed in the spectrum and beyond the violet causes a visible prolongation of the spectrum. The light in the newly-seen and once invisible part of the spectrum is yellow, the colour of the ribbon itself. In fact, the whole of that part of the spectrum, which on the white screen is seen as blue and violet, becomes yellow, the red and green remaining unchanged. This change in colour is due to fluorescence, a phenomenon of light which Sir G. Stokes found was caused by an alteration in the lengths of the waves of light when reflected from certain bodies. It is not meant to imply by this that the wave-length of any ray falling on a body can be altered by reflection, but only that the body itself on which the rays fall emits rays of light which are not of the same wave-length as those which fall upon it. Now it is a fact that the rays that lie beyond the violet, and which are ordinarily invisible, are shorter than the violet rays, and that these are shorter than the yellow rays. It follows therefore that when, what we may now call, the ultra-violet rays fall on the yellow dyed ribbon, the waves emitted by it are so lengthened that they appear yellow to the eye instead of dark, violet, or blue.

We can also brush a solution of quinine on the screen, and immediately the place where the ultra-violet rays fall is illuminated by a violet light. We do not see the ultra-violet rays themselves, but only the rays of increased wave-length, which are emitted by their effect on the sulphate of quinine. Common machine oil as used for engines also emits greenish rays when excited by the ultra-violet rays, and a very beautiful colour it is. Fluorescence then is one means of demonstrating the existence of the ultra-violet rays—or Ritter's rays as they were formerly called, after their discoverer—in a very simple manner. The method of rendering the effects of the infra-red rays visible to the eye is also interesting. All, or at all events most, of our readers have seen Balmain's luminous paint. A glass or card coated with this substance, which is essentially a sulphide of calcium, when exposed to the light of the sun, or of the electric arc, and then taken into comparative darkness, is seen to shine with a peculiar violet-coloured light. If when thus excited we place it in a bright spectrum for some little time, we shall find on shutting off the light that where the ultra-violet and blue fell on it, the violet light is intenser than the light of the main part of the screen; where the yellow fell there is neither increase or diminution in brightness; but that in the red it becomes darker, and also beyond the limit of the visible spectrum, indicating the existence of rays beyond, which through their greater length have not the power of affecting the eye. If the spectrum be shut off, however, very soon after it falls on the plate, it has been asserted that the red and infra-red rays have increased the brightness of that particular part of the plate on which they fell. At first these two observations seem to contradict one another; they do not in reality. We may expose a tablet of Balmain's paint to light, and place a heated iron in contact with the back of the plate; we shall then find that the iron produces a bright image of its surface on a less bright background. This bright image will gradually fade away, and the same space will eventually become dark compared with the rest of the plate. The reason of this is clear. When light excites the paint a certain amount of energy is poured into it, which it radiates out slowly as light. When the hot iron is placed in contact with it, the heat causes the light to radiate more rapidly, and consequently with greater intensity, at the part where its surface touches, and the energy of that particular portion becomes used up. When the energy of radiation of this part becomes less than that of the rest of the tablet, its light must of necessity be of less brightness than that of the background, with which the heated iron has had no contact. For this reason the image of the iron subsequently appears dark. We shall see presently, and as before stated, that the principal heating effect of the spectrum lies in the red and infra-red, and it is owing to the heating of the paint by these rays that the image might be at first slightly brighter than the background, and subsequently darker.

There is another way in which the existence of both the ultra-violet and infra-red rays can be demonstrated, and that is by means of photography. If we place an ordinary photographic plate in the spectrum and develop it, we shall find that besides being affected by the blue and violet rays, it is also affected by the rays beyond the violet, the energy of these rays being capable of causing a decomposition of the sensitive silver salt. If quartz prisms and lenses be used, and the electric light be the source of illumination, the ultra-violet spectrum will extend to an enormous extent. A more difficult, but perhaps even more interesting means of illustrating the existence of the infra-red rays, and first due to the writer, can be made by means of photography. It is possible to prepare a photographic plate with bromide of silver, which is so molecularly arranged that it becomes capable of being decomposed not only by the violet and blue rays, but also by the red rays, and by those rays which have wave-lengths of nearly three times that of the red rays. It would be inappropriate to enter into a description of the method of the preparation of these plates. Those who are curious as to it will find a description in the Bakerian lecture published in the Philosophical Transactions of the Royal Society for 1881. With plates so prepared it has been found possible to obtain impressions in the dark with the rays coming from a black object, heated to only a black heat.

That these dark rays possess greater energy or capacity for doing work of some kind than any other rays of the spectrum, can be shown by means of a linear thermopile (Fig. 4), if it be so arranged as to allow only a narrow vertical slice of light to reach its face.

FIG. 4.
The Thermopile.

The principle of the thermopile we need not describe in detail. Suffice it to say that the heating of the soldered junctions of two dissimilar metals (there are ten pairs of antimony and bismuth in the above instrument) produces a feeble current of electricity, which, however, is sufficient to cause a deflection to the suspended needle of a delicate galvanometer. To the needle is attached a mirror weighing a fraction of a grain, and the deflections are made visible by the reflection from it of a beam of light issuing from a fixed point along a scale. The greater the heating of the junctions of the thermopile, within limits which in these cases are never exceeded, the greater is the current produced, and consequently the greater is the deflection of the mirror-bearing needle, and of the beam of light along the scale. In order to get a comparative measure of the energies of the different rays, it is necessary that they should be completely absorbed. Now the junctions themselves of the pile being metal, and therefore more or less bright, will not absorb completely, but if they be coated with a fine layer of lamp-black, the rays falling on the pile will be absorbed by this substance, and their absorption will cause a rise in temperature in it, and the heat will be communicated to the thermopile.

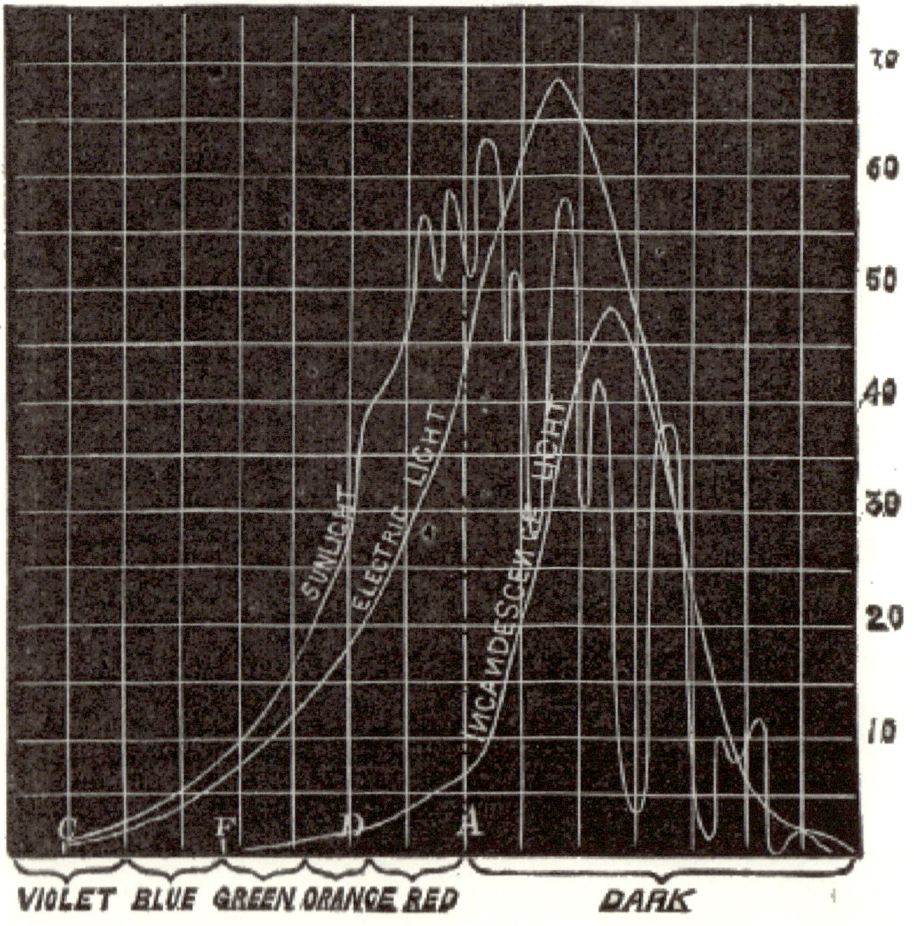

FIG. 5.
Heating effect of different Sources of Radiation.

If we make a bright spectrum, and one not too long, say three inches in length, and pass the linear thermopile through its length, we shall find that when the galvanometer is attached, the galvanometer needle will be differently deflected in its various parts. The deflection will be almost insensible in the violet, but sensible in the blue, rather more in the green, still more in the yellow, and it will further increase in the red. When, however, the slit of the thermopile is placed beyond the limit of the visible spectrum, the deflection enormously increases, and will increase till a position is reached as far below the red as the yellow is above it. After this maximum is reached, by moving the pile still further from the red, the galvanometer needle will travel towards its zero, and finally all deflection will cease. At this point we may suppose we have reached the limit of the spectrum, but if rock-salt prisms and lenses be used, the limit will be increased. What the real limit of the spectrum is, is at present unknown; Mr. Langley with his bolometer, and rock-salt prisms, an instrument more sensitive than the thermopile, must have nearly reached it.

The above figure is a graphic representation of the heating effect of the spectrum of the electric light, sunlight, and the incandescence electric light, on the lamp-black coating of the thermopile, as shown by the galvanometer. The vast difference between the heating effect of the visible rays of the first two sources compared with the last is clearly indicated.

Since every ray may be taken as totally absorbed, the heating of the lamp-black is a measure of the energy or the capacity of performing work of some description, which they possess. Waves of the sea do work when they beat against the shore, and they do work when they lift a vessel. If we notice a ship at anchor we shall find that behind the vessel and towards the shore the waves are lowered in height or amplitude; the energy which they have expended in raising the vessel of necessity causes this lowering. In the same way the waves of light, after falling on matter whose molecules or atoms are swinging in unison with them, are destroyed, and the energy is spent in either decomposing the matter into a simpler form at first—though the subsequent form may be more complex—or in raising its temperature. As lamp-black or carbon is in its simplest form, the only work done upon it by the energy of radiation is the raising of its temperature, and it is for this reason that this material is so excellent for covering the junctions of the pile. The eye evidently does not absorb all rays, since only a limited part of the spectrum is visible, and it would be useless to take a measure of the heating effect of lamp-black for the visible part of the spectrum as a measure of its luminosity, since the latter fades off in the red—the very place in which the heat curve rises rapidly.

CHAPTER IV.

Description of Colour Patch Apparatus—Rotating Sectors—Method
of making a Scale for the Spectrum.

Before proceeding further we must describe somewhat in detail two or three pieces of apparatus to be used in the experiments we shall make.

The first piece was devised by the writer a few years ago, and has got rid of several objections which existed in older pieces of apparatus. It is not only useful for lecture purposes, but also for careful laboratory work. The ordinary lecture apparatus for throwing a spectrum on the screen is of too crude a form to be effective for the purpose we have in view; the purity of the colours seen on the screen is more than doubtful, and this alone unfits it for our experiments. If we want to form a pure spectrum we must have a narrow slit, prisms with true, flat surfaces, and lenses of proper curvature. As a rule the ordinary lecture apparatus for forming the spectrum lacks all of these requisites.

The accompanying diagram (Fig. 6) will give an idea of the apparatus we shall employ. On the usual slit S_1 of a collimator C is thrown, by means of a condensing lens L_1, a beam of light, which emanates from the intensely white-hot carbon positive pole of the electric light. The focus is so adjusted that an image of the crater is formed on the slit. The collimating lens L_2 is filled by this beam, and the rays issue parallel to one another and fall on the prisms P_1 and P_2, which disperse them. The dispersed beam falls on a corrected photographic lens L_3, attached to a camera in the ordinary way. It is of slightly larger diameter than the height of the prisms, and a spectrum is formed on the focusing-screen D, which is slewed at a slight angle with the perpendicular to the axis of the lens L_3. This is necessary, because the focus of the least refrangible or red rays is longer than that of the more refrangible or blue rays. By slewing the focusing-screen as shown, a very good general focus for every ray may be obtained. When the focusing-screen is removed, the rays form a confused patch of parti-coloured light on a white screen F, placed some four feet off the camera. The rays, however, can be collected by a lens L_4, of about two feet focus, placed near the position of the focusing-screen, and slightly askew. This forms an image on the screen of the near surface of the last prism P_2; and if correctly adjusted, the rectangular patch of light should be pure and without any fringes of colour. The card D slides into the grooves which ordinarily take the dark slide. In it will be seen a slit S_2, the utility of which will be explained later on.

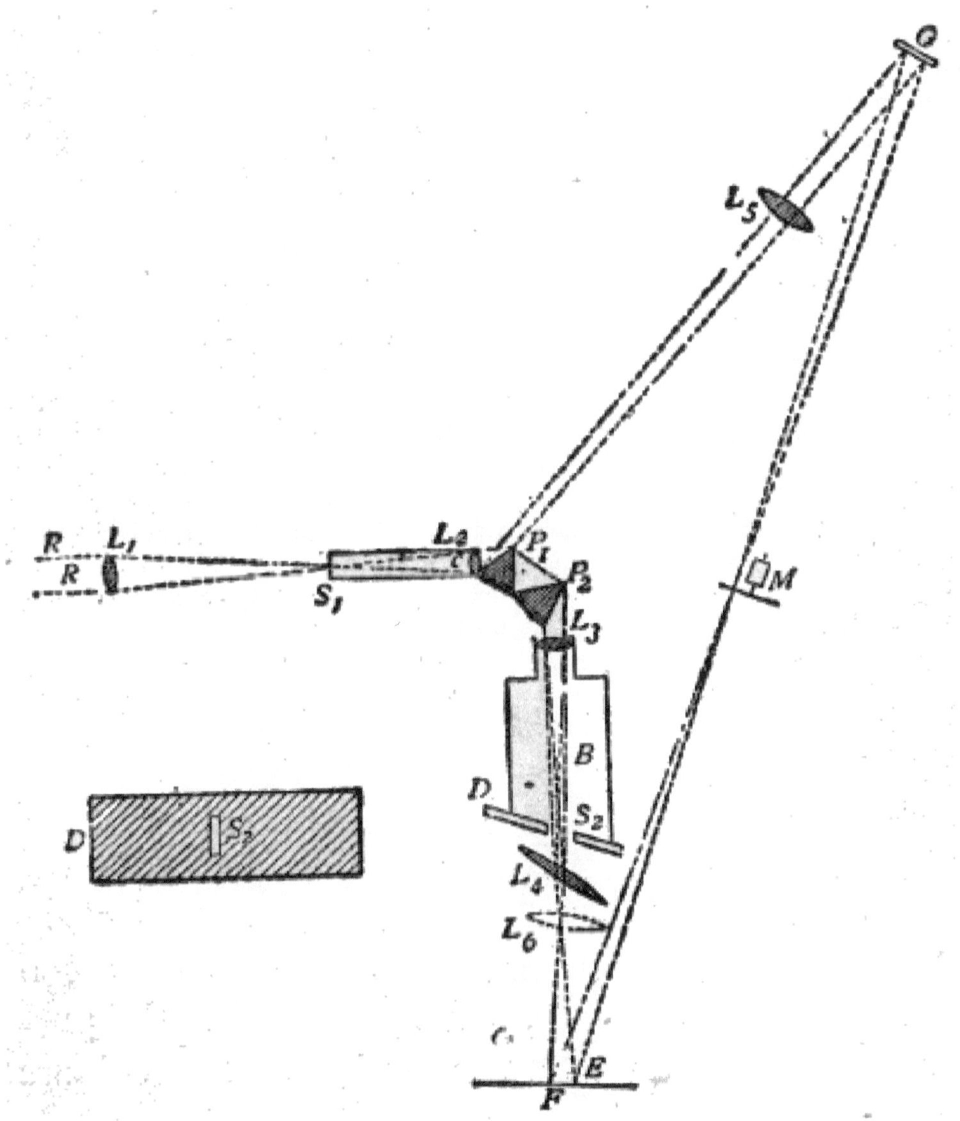

FIG. 6.
Colour Patch Apparatus.

We shall usually require a second patch of white light, with which to compare the first patch. Now, although the light from the positive pole of the carbons is uniform in quality, it sometimes varies in quantity, as it is difficult to keep its image always in exactly the centre of the slit. If we can take one part of the light coming through the slit to form the spectrum, and another part to form the second patch of white light, then the brightness of the two will vary together. At first sight this might appear difficult to attain; but advantage is taken of the fact that from the first surface of the first prism P_1 a certain amount of light is reflected. Placing a lens L_5, and a mirror G, in the path of this reflected beam, another square patch of light can be thrown on the same screen as that on which the first is thrown, and this second patch may be made of the same size as the first patch, if the lens L_5 be of suitable focus, and it can be superposed over the first patch if required; or, as is useful in some cases, the two patches may be placed side by side, just touching each other.

We are thus able to secure two square white patches upon the screen F, one from the re-combination of the spectrum, and one from the reflected beam. If a rod be placed in the path of these two beams when they are superposed, each beam will throw a shadow of the rod upon the screen. The shadow cast by the integrated spectrum will be illuminated by the reflected beam, and the shadow cast by the latter will be illuminated by the former. In fact we have an ordinary Rumford photometer, and the two shadows may be caused to touch one another by moving the rod towards or from the screen. When the illumination of the two shadows by the white light is equal, the whole should appear as *one* unbroken gray patch. To prevent confusion to the eye a black mask is placed on the screen F with a square aperture cut out of it, on which the two shadows are caused to fall. If it be desired to diminish the brightness of either patch, it can be accomplished by the introduction of rotating sectors M, which can be opened and closed at pleasure during rotation, in the path of one or other of the beams.

FIG. 7.
Rotating Sectors.

The annexed figure (Fig. 7) is a bird's-eye view of the instrument. A A are two sectors, one of which is capable of closing the open aperture by means of a lever arrangement C, which moves a sleeve in which is fixed a pin working in a screw groove, which allows the aperture in the sectors to be opened and closed at pleasure during their revolution; D is an electro-motor causing the sectors to rotate. To show its efficiency, if two strips of paper, one coated with lamp-black and the other white, are placed side by side on the screen, and if one shadow from the rod falls on the white strip, and the other shadow on the black strip of paper, and the rotating sectors are interposed in the path of the light illuminating the shadow cast on the white strip, the aperture of the sectors can be closed till the white paper appears absolutely blacker than the black paper. White thus becomes darker than lamp-black, owing to the want of illumination. This is an interesting experiment, and we shall see its bearings as we proceed, as it indicates that even lamp-black reflects a certain amount of white or other light.

Having thus explained the main part of the apparatus with which we shall work, we can go on and show how monochromatic light of any degree of purity can be produced on the screen. If the slit in the cardboard slide D be passed through the spectrum when it has been focused on the focusing-screen, only one small strip of practically monochromatic light will reach the screen, and instead of the white patch on the screen we shall have a succession of coloured patches, the colour varying according to the position the slit occupies in the spectrum. It should be noted that the purity of the colour depends on two things—the narrowness of the slit S_1 of the collimator, and of the slit S_2 in the card. If two slits be cut in the card D, we shall have two coloured patches overlapping one another, and if the reflected beam falls on the same space we shall have a mixture of coloured light with white light, and either the coloured light or the white light can be reduced in brightness by the introduction of the rotating sectors. If the rod be introduced in the path of the rays we shall have two shadows cast, one illuminated with coloured light, monochromatic or compound, and the other with white light, and these can be placed side by side, and surrounded by the black mask as before described.

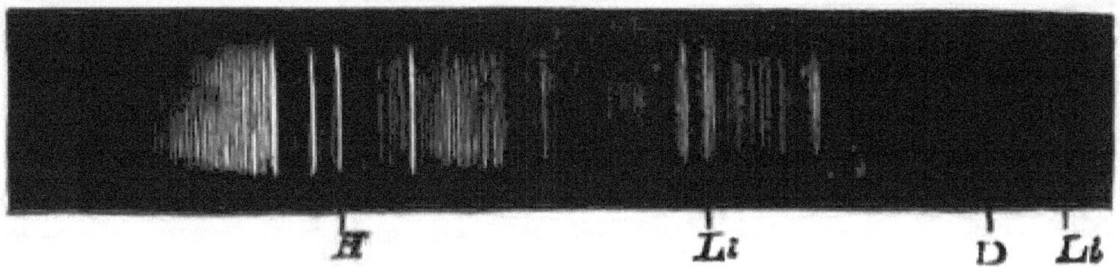

FIG. 8.
Spectrum of Sodium Lithium and Carbon.

There is one other part of the apparatus which may be mentioned, and that is the indicator, which tells us what part of the spectrum is passing through the slit. Just outside the camera, and in a line with the focusing-screen, is a clip carrying a vertical needle. A small beam of light passes outside the prism P_1; this is caught by a mirror attached to the side of the apparatus, and is reflected so as to cast a shadow of the needle on to the back of the card D, on which a carefully divided scale of twentieths of an inch is drawn. To fix the position of the slit the poles of the electric light are brushed over with a solution of the carbonates of sodium and lithium in hydrochloric acid, and the image of the arc is thrown on the slit. This gets rid of the continuous spectrum, and only the bright lines due to the incandescent vapours appear on the focusing-screen (Fig. 8). Amongst other lines we have the red and blue lines due to the vapour of lithium; the orange, yellow (D), and green lines of sodium, together with the violet lines of calcium (these last due to the impurities of the carbons forming the poles). These lines are caused successively to fall on the centre of the slit by moving the card D, which for the nonce is covered with a piece of ground glass, and the position of the shadow of the needle-point on the scale is registered for each. A further check can be made by taking a photograph of these lines, or of the solar spectrum, and having fixed accurately on the scale any one of these lines already named, the position of the others on the scale may be ascertained by measurement from the photograph. Now the wave-lengths of these bright lines have been most accurately ascertained, in fact as accurately as the dark lines in the solar spectrum. Thus the scale on the card is a means of localizing the colour passing through the slit or slits. Should more than one slit be used in the spectrum the positions of each can be determined in exactly the same way. The most tedious part of the whole experimental arrangement with this apparatus is what may be called the scaling of the spectrum.

A fairly large spectrum may be formed upon the screen without altering any arrangement of the apparatus, when it has been adjusted to form colour patches. If a lens L_6 (see Fig. 6) of short focus be placed in front of L_4 (the big combining lens), an enlarged spectrum will be thrown upon the screen F, and if slits be placed in the spectrum the images of their apertures are formed by the respective coloured rays passing through them, so that the colours which are combined in the patch can be immediately seen.

CHAPTER V.

Absorption of the Spectrum—Analysis of Colour—Vibrations of Rays—Absorption by Pigments—Phosphorescence—Interference.

We must now briefly consider what is the origin, or at all events the cause, of the colour which we see in objects. It is not proposed to enter into this by any means minutely, but only sufficiently to enable us to understand the subject which is to be brought before you. What for instance is the cause of the colour of this green solution of chlorophyll, which is an extract of cabbage leaves? If we place it in the front of the spectrum apparatus and throw the spectrum on the screen, we find that while there is a certain amount of blue transmitted, the green is strong, and there are red bands left, but a good deal of the spectrum is totally absorbed. Forming a colour patch of this absorption spectrum on the screen, we see that it is the same colour as the chlorophyll solution, and of this we can judge more accurately by using the reflected beam, and placing the rod in position to cast shadows. (The light of the reflected beam is that of the light entering the slit.) The colour then of the chlorophyll is due to the absence of certain colours from the spectrum of white light. When white light passes through it, the material absorbs, or filters out, some of the coloured rays, and allows others to pass more or less unaffected, and it is the re-combination of these last which makes up the colour of the chlorophyll. We have a green dye which to the eye is very similar in colour to chlorophyll, but putting a solution of it in front of the spectrum, we see that it cuts off different rays to the latter. It would be quite possible to mistake one green for the other, but directly we analyze the white light which has filtered through each by means of the spectrum, we at once see that they differ. Hence the spectrum enables the eye to discriminate by analysis what it would otherwise be unable to do. Any coloured solution or transparent body may be analyzed in the same way, and, as we shall see subsequently, the intensity of every ray after passing through it can be accurately compared with the original incident light. There are some cases, indeed the majority of cases, in which the colour transmitted through a small thickness of the material is different to that transmitted through a greater thickness. For instance, a weak solution of litmus in water is blue when a thin layer is examined, and red when it is a thicker or more concentrated layer. Bichromate of potash is more ruddy as the thickness increases. This can be readily understood by a reference to the law of absorption. Suppose we have a thin layer of a liquid which gives a purple colour when two simple colours, red and blue, pass through it, and that this thin layer cuts off one-quarter of the red and one-half of the blue incident on it, another layer of equal thickness will cut off another quarter of the three-quarters of red passing through the first layer, and half of the one-half left of the blue; we shall thus have nine-sixteenths of the red passing and only a quarter of the blue. With a third layer we shall have twenty-seven sixty-fourths of red and only one-eighth of blue left, showing that as the thickness of the liquid is increased the blue rapidly disappears, leaving the red the dominant colour. Now what is true of two simple colours is equally true of any number of them, where the rates of absorption differ from one another, and what is true for a solution is true for a transparent solid. In some opaque bodies, such as rocks, the reflected colour often differs slightly from that of the same when they are cut into thin and polished slices, through which the light can pass. The reason is that when opaque, light penetrates to a very small distance through the surface, and is reflected back, whilst in these layers the colour has to struggle through more coloured matter, and emerges of a different hue.

The question why substances transmit some rays and quench others, brings us into the domain of molecular physics. Of all branches of physical science this is perhaps the most fascinating and the most speculative, yet it is one which is being built up on the solid foundations of experiment and mathematics, till it has attained an importance which the questions depending on it fully warrants. We have to picture to ourselves, in the case in point, molecules, and the atoms composing them, of a size which no microscope can bring to view, vibrating in certain definite periods which are similar to the periods of oscillation of the waves of light. At page 26 we have given the lengths of some of the waves which give the sensation of coloured light. Now as light, of whatever colour it may be, is practically transmitted with the same velocity through air which has the same density throughout, it follows that the number of vibrations per second of each ray can be obtained by dividing the velocity of light in any medium by the wave-length. The following table gives roughly the number of vibrations per second of the ether giving rise to the colours fixed by the dark solar lines.

Name of Line.	Millions of Millions of; Vibrations per Second.
A in the Red	395
B in the Red	437
C in the Red	458
D in the Orange	510
E in the Green	570
F in the Blue	618
G in the Violet	697
H in the Ultra-Violet	757

If we endeavour to gauge what this rate of oscillation means we shall scarcely be able to realize it, even by a comparison with some physically measurable rate of vibration. A tuning-fork, for instance, giving the middle C, vibrates 528 times per second. Compare this with the number of vibrations of the waves of light, and we still are as far as ever from realizing it, yet the velocity of light, and the lengths of the different waves have been accurately determined; the latter, although the much smaller quantity, with even greater accuracy than the first. These rates of vibration must therefore be—cannot help being—at all events approximately true. This being so, we know that some of the atoms of the molecules at least, and perhaps in some cases the molecules themselves, are vibrating at the same rate as those waves of light, which they refuse to allow to pass. If we have a child's swing beginning to oscillate, we know that it is only by well-timed blows that the extent of the swing is permanently increased, and the energy exerted by the person who gives the well-timed blow is expended on producing the increased amplitude. In the same way if the rate of vibration of a wave of light is in accord with that of a molecule or atom, the amplitude or swing of the atom or molecule is increased, and the energy of the wave and therefore its amplitude is totally or partially destroyed; and as the amplitude is a function of the intensity of the light, the ray fails to be seen at all, or else is diminished in brightness.

In what way the atoms vibrate where more than one ray is absorbed is still a matter of speculation, but no doubt as experimental methods are more fully developed, and mathematicians investigate the results of such experiments, we shall be able to form a picture of the vibrations themselves. At page 137 a speculation as to the reason why solids or liquids can absorb more waves of light than one which are adjacent to each other is put forward, but it does not deal with the absorptions which occupy various parts of the spectrum. Again, too, we have the fact that the energy absorbed by these atoms and molecules from the waves of light, must show itself as work done on them—it may be as heat or as chemical action. We shall see by and by that in some cases, no doubt, at least a part is expended in the latter form of work.

Perhaps this mode of looking at the question of colour in objects may make the subject more interesting to the reader than it at first appears to be deserving. The whole subject is one which enlarges the faculty of making mental pictures, and this is one of the most useful forms of scientific education.

But how can we distinguish between pigments which to the eye are apparently the same? If we dye paper with the green dye referred to, we can place it in the spectrum, and we shall see that the dye reflects differently to the white paper. In fact we shall find that it refuses to reflect in those parts of the spectrum which the transparent solution refused to transmit. So long as the light passes through the dye-stuff, it is indifferent, as regards the colour produced, whether the colouring matter be at a distance from the paper or whether the latter be dyed with it, as we can see at once. If we place the solution of the dye in the reflected beam of the apparatus and form a patch on the screen, and alongside throw the patch of white light from the integrated or recombined spectrum upon the dyed paper, it will be found that the two colours are alike; that is, the green-coloured light on the white paper, or the white light on the green paper are the same. Similarly we may experiment on other dyes, such as magenta, log-wood, &c., and we shall see that like results are obtained. It should be said, however, that when the paper is dyed with the colouring matter a *small quantity* of white light will be reflected from the surface of the paper itself. We may now say that the general colour is given to a body by its refusal to transmit or reflect, more or less completely, certain rays of the spectrum. Should the solvent form a compound with the dye, perhaps this would not be absolutely true, but in the large majority of cases the statement is correct. When we have bodies which are also fluorescent, this statement would also have to be modified, but we need not consider these for the present.

Another source of colour in objects, though very rarely met with, and which for our object we need not stay to explain in detail, is the interference of light. Such is seen in soap-bubbles. Briefly it may be said that the colours are due to rays of light reflected from the inner surface of the film, which quench other rays of light of the same wave-length reflected from the outer surface. If two series of waves of the same wave-length are going in the same direction and from the same source, each of which has the same intensity as the other, that is, having the same amplitude, and it happens that the one series is exactly half a wave-length behind the other, then the crest of one wave in the first series will fill up the trough of the other in the second series, and no motion would result, and this lack of motion means darkness, since it is the wave motion which gives the sensation of light. If then we have white light falling on two reflecting surfaces, such as the front and back of a soap-film, part of the light will be reflected from each, and if the film be of such a thickness that the latter reflects light exactly ½ wave-length, 3/2 or 5/2 wave-length, &c., of some colour behind the former, the colour due to that particular wave-length will be absent from the reflected white light, and instead of white light we shall have coloured light, due to the combination of all the colours less this colour, which is quenched.

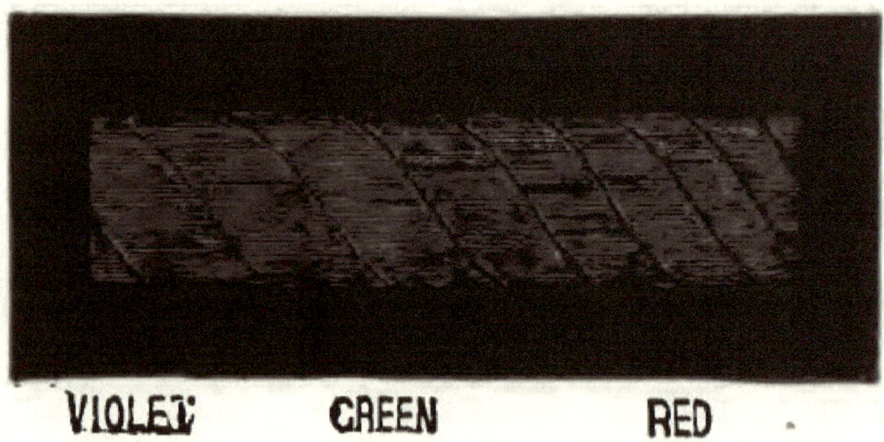

FIG. 9.
Interference Bands.

A very pretty experiment to make is to throw the image of a soap film on the screen, and to watch the change in the colours of the film. Their brilliancy increases as the film becomes thinner, and the bands, which first appear close to each other, separate, and then we see a large expanse of changing colour. A soap solution should be made according to almost any of the published formulæ, and a piece of flat card be dipped in it, and be drawn across a ring of wire some inch in diameter, or—what the writer prefers best—the stop of a photographic lens. A film will form and fill the aperture. The ring or stop may be placed vertically in a clamp, and a beam of light caused to fall at an angle of about 45 degrees on to the film. If a lens be placed in the path of the reflected beam to form an image of the aperture, the colours which the film shows can be exhibited to an audience, if the diameter of the image be made four or five feet. Instead of this large image, a small image may be thrown on the slit of the spectroscope, by using a lens of a greater focal length, and if the beam be so directed that it falls on the axis of the collimator, a very fairly bright spectrum may be also thrown on the screen. The appearance of the spectrum is somewhat like that shown in the above diagram (Fig. 9).

If we take a horizontal line across the spectrum, we shall see what particular colours are missing from the reflected light which falls on the part of the slit corresponding to that line. The colours of some objects, such as of the opal, and the lovely colouring of some feathers are due to interference of light. The partial scattering of different rays by small particles will also cause light to be coloured, as we shall see in the experiments we shall make to imitate the colour of sunlight at various altitudes of the sun. We may, however, take it as a rule that the colour of objects is produced by the greater or less absorption of some rays, and the reflection in the case of opaque bodies, or the transmission, in the case of transparent bodies, of the remainder.

CHAPTER VI.

Scattered Light—Sunset Colours—Law of the Scattering by Fine Particles—Sunset Clouds—Luminosities of Sunlight at different Altitudes of the Sun.

It is probable that we should be able to ascertain approximately the true colour of sunlight (if we may talk of the colour of white light) if we could collect all the light from a cloudless sky, and condense it on a patch of sunlight thrown on a screen. For skylight is, after all, only a portion of the light of the sun, scattered from small particles in the atmosphere, part of the light being scattered into space, and part to our earth. The small particles of water and dust—and when we say small we mean small when measured on the same scale as we measure the lengths of waves of light—differentiate between waves of different lengths, and scatter the blue rays more than the green, and the green than the red; consequently what the sun lacks in blue and green is to be found in the light of the sky. The effect that small water particles have upon light passing through them can be very well seen in the streets of London at night, when the atmosphere is at all foggy. Gaslights at the far end of a street appear to become ruby red and dim, and half-way down only orange, but brighter, whilst close to they are of the ordinary yellow colour, and of normal brightness. When no fog is present the gas-lights in the distance and close to are of the same colour and brightness, showing that their change in appearance is simply due to the misty atmosphere intervening between them and the observer. We can imitate the light from the sun, after its passage through various thicknesses of atmosphere, in a very perfect manner in the lecture-room, using the electric light as a source. A condensing lens is put in front of the lamp, and in front of that a circular aperture in a plate. Beyond that again is a lens which throws an enlarged image of the aperture on the screen, which we may call our mock sun. If we place a trough of glass, in which is a dilute solution of hyposulphite of soda, carefully filtered from motes as far as possible, in front of the aperture, we have an image of the aperture unaffected by the insertion of the solution. The white disc on the screen will, as we have said before, be a close approximation to sunlight on a May-day about noon, when the sky is clear. By dropping into the trough a little dilute hydrochloric acid, a change will be found to come over the light of the mock sun; a pale yellow colour will spread over its surface, and this will give way to an orange tint, and at the same time its brightness will diminish. Gradually the orange will give place to red, the luminosity will be very small, being of the same hue as that seen in the sun when viewed through a London fog. Finally the last trace of red will so mingle with the scattered white light that the image will disappear, and then the experiment is over.

If we track the cause of this change of colour in our artificial sun, we shall find that it is due to minute particles of sulphur separating out from the solution of hyposulphite, and the longer the time that elapses the more turbid the dilute solution will become. This experiment exemplifies the action of small particles on light. Examining the trough it will be found that whilst the light which passes *through the solution* principally loses blue rays, the light which is scattered from the sides is almost cerulean in blue, and can well be compared with the light from the sky. We can analyze the transmitted light very readily by focusing the beam from the positive pole of the electric light on to the slit of our colour apparatus, and placing the lens L_6 (Fig. 6) in position to form the large spectrum on the screen. We can also show the colour of the light which goes to form the spectrum, by sending the patch of light reflected from the first surface of the first prism just above it. We thus have the spectrum and the light forming the spectrum to compare with one another. Using this apparatus and inserting the trough of dilute hyposulphite in the beam, the spectrum is of the character usually seen with the electric light; but on dropping the dilute hydrochloric acid into the solution the same hues fall on the slit of the spectroscope which fell upon the screen to form the mock sun, and the spectrum is seen to change as the light changes from white to yellow, and from yellow to red. First the violet will disappear, the blue and the green being dimmed, the former most however; then the blue will vanish to the eye, the green becoming still less luminous, and the yellow also fading; the green and yellow will successively disappear, leaving finally on the screen a red band alone, which will be a near match to the colour of the unanalyzed light, as may be seen by comparing it with the adjacent patch formed from the reflected beam.

We have here a proof that the succession of phenomena is caused by a scattering of the shorter wave-lengths of light, and that the shorter the waves are the more they are scattered. It has been found theoretically by Lord Rayleigh that the scattering takes place in inverse proportion to the fourth power of the wavelength; thus, if two wave-lengths, which may be waves in the green and violet, are in the proportion of three to four, the former will be scattered as $1/3^4$ to $1/4^4$, or as 256 to 81, which is approximately as three to one. Consequently if the green in passing through a certain thickness of a turbid medium loses one-half the violet in passing through the same thickness will lose five-sixths of its luminosity. The inverse fourth powers of the following wave-lengths, which are within the limits of the whole visible spectrum, are shown below.

λ	7000	6000	5000	4000
$1/\lambda^4$	1	·504	·260	·107

Supposing $\lambda 7000$ by the scattering of small particles loses one-tenth of its luminosity, then $\lambda 6000$ would have ·454 of its original brightness; $\lambda 5000$, ·234; and $\lambda 4000$, ·095; that is, whilst $\lambda 7000$ would lose one-tenth only of its luminosity, $\lambda 4000$ in the violet would retain not quite one-hundredth of its brightness.

During the years 1885, 1886, and 1887, the writer measured the luminosity of the solar spectrum at different times of the year, and at different hours of the day (see *Phil. Trans.* 1887: "Transmission of Sunlight through the Earth's Atmosphere"), and from the results he found that the smallest coefficient of scattering for one atmosphere at sea-level for each wave-length was ·0013, when λ^{-4} was for convenience sake multiplied by 10^{17} (thus $\lambda6000^{-4}$ on this scale was 77·2), and that the mean was ·0017.

Line.	Wave-length.	$1/\lambda^{-4}$ $\times 10^{17}$	Light after passing through atmospheres of the following thicknesses.									
			0	1	2	3	4	5	6	7	8	32
A	7594	30	1	·955	·908	·857	·815	·775	·736	·707	·665	·107
B	6867	45	1	·926	·858	·795	·735	·684	·632	·583	·542	·086
C	6562	54	1	·912	·832	·759	·693	·632	·576	·526	·480	·019
D	5892	83	1	·868	·754	·655	·569	·494	·428	·372	·323	·001
E	5269	129	1	·803	·644	·518	·427	·334	·268	·216	·173	—
F	4861	179	1	·738	·544	·402	·296	·219	·161	·119	·088	—
G	4307	291	1	·609	·367	·220	·137	·084	·051	·031	·019	—
H	3968	403	1	·506	·254	·128	·071	·033	·016	·008	·004	—

The following table shows the loss of light for the rays denoted by the principal lines given at page 26, using this last coefficient for different air thicknesses. This is equivalent to giving the intensity of the rays of sunlight when the sun is at different altitudes.

The sun traverses the following thicknesses of atmosphere when it is at the angles shown above the horizon.

1	atmosphere	90°
2	atmosphere	30°
3	atmosphere	19·30
4	atmosphere	14·30
5	atmosphere	11·30
6	atmosphere	9·30
7	atmosphere	8·30
8	atmosphere	7·30

It traverses thirty-two atmospheres when it is very nearly setting. Bougier and Forbes have calculated that the extreme thickness of the atmosphere, traversed by its light when the sun is on the horizon, is approximately 35½ atmospheres. The absorption shown by 32 atmospheres will therefore be very close to that which would be observed at sunset on an ordinary day, and it will be seen that practically all rays have been scattered from the light, except the red, and a little bit of the orange.

As to the luminosity of the sun at these different altitudes, we can easily find it by reducing the luminosity curve of the sun at some known altitude by the factors in the table just given, for as many wave-lengths as we please, and thus construct another curve. The area of the figure thus obtained would be a measure of the total luminosity on the same scale as the area of the luminosity curve from which it was derived.

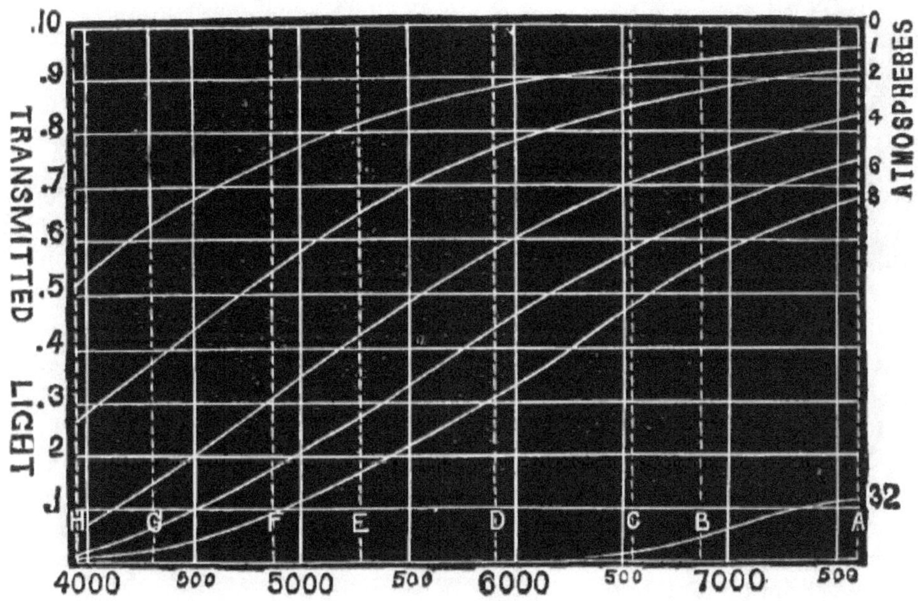

FIG. 10.
Absorption of Rays by the Atmosphere.

The following are the approximate luminosities of the sun when the light shines

through	0	atmospheres	1
through	1	atmospheres	·840
through	2	atmospheres	·705
through	3	atmospheres	·594
through	4	atmospheres	·496
through	5	atmospheres	·417
through	6	atmospheres	·303
through	7	atmospheres	·256
through	8	atmospheres	·215
through	32	atmospheres	·002

It will thus be seen that the sun is 420 times less bright just at sunset than it is if it were to shine directly overhead, and about 350 times brighter than it is for a winter sun in a cloudless and mistless sky at twelve o'clock, for the altitude of the sun in our latitude is about 30° at that time, and corresponds with a thickness of two atmospheres, through which the sun has to shine. We all know that to look at the sun at any time near noon in a cloudless sky dazzles the eyes, but that near sunset it may be looked at with impunity. The reduction in luminosity explains this fact.

The distribution of the scattering particles in the atmosphere is very far from regular. As we ascend, the particles get more sparse, as is shown by the less scattering that takes place of the blue rays compared with the red. Thus at an altitude of some 8000 feet the mean coefficient of scattering is about ·0003, instead of ·0017, which it is at sea-level. It must be recollected that there is only about three-fourths of the air above us at 8000 feet, and it is less dense. There will therefore be a diminution of particles not only because there is less air, but because the air itself is less capable of keeping them in suspension. Up to 3000 or 4000 feet there is no very great marked difference in the scattering of light, as observations carried on during five years have shown; but above that the scattering rapidly diminishes, and at 20,000 feet it must be very small indeed, if the diminution increases as rapidly as has been found it does at the altitude of 8000 feet.

We must repeat once more that the blue of the sky is principally if not entirely due to the presence of these particles, the rays scattered by them, which are principally the blue rays, being reflected back from them, giving the sensation of blue which we know as sky-blue. The greater the number of these fine particles that are encountered by sunlight, the greater the scattering will be, and the bluer the sky. It is more than probable that the blue sky of Italy, so proverbial for being beautiful, is due to this cause, since from its geographical position the small particles of water must be very abundant there.

Carrying this argument further, we should expect that as we mount higher the blue would become more fully mixed with the darkness of space, and this Alpine travellers will tell you is the case. At heights of 12,000 feet or more, on a clear day, the sky seems almost black, and it is no uncommon thing to see this admirably rendered in photographs of Alpine scenery when taken at a height. Many of the late Mr. Donkin's photographs show this in great perfection, as also Signor Sella's.

Before quitting this subject we may call attention not only to the colour of the sun itself at sunset, but also to the colouring of the sky which accompanies the sun as it sinks. This colouring is often different to the colour that the sun itself assumes; but we can easily show that the effects so wonderfully beautiful are entirely dependent on this scattering of light by these small intervening particles in the air. We often see a ruddy sun, and perhaps nearly in the zenith, or even further away from the sun, clouds of a beautiful crimson hue, lying on a sky which appears almost pea-green, whilst nearer to the sun the sky is a brilliant orange, which artists imitate with cadmium yellow. Let us fix our attention first on the crimson cloud. The clouds of which the colouring is so gorgeous are often not 1000 feet above us, and were we to be at that altitude we should see the sun not quite so ruddy as we see it from the earth, and the cloud would consequently be illuminated by the sun with a more orange tint; but the light reflected from the cloud to our eyes has to pass through, say 1000 feet of dense atmosphere, and thus the total atmosphere that the light traverses in the latter case is always greater than the air thickness through which the direct light from the sun has to pass; hence more orange is cut off, and the light reflected from the cloud is redder. This red, however, will not account for the brilliant crimson and purples which we so often see. It has to be remembered that not sunlight alone illumines the cloud, but also the blue light of the sky. The feebler the intensity of the red, the more will the blue of the sky be felt in the mixture of light which reaches our eyes, and consequently we may have any tint ranging from crimson to purple, since red and blue make these hues, according to the proportions in which they are mixed.

Now let us see how we get the brilliant orange of the sky itself. When the evening is perfectly clear and free from mist and cloud, the orange in the sky is very feeble, showing that the intensity depends upon their presence. Now a look at the table will show that the sun is very close to the horizon when it becomes ruddy under normal conditions; but that when the light traverses a thickness of eight atmospheres, the blue and violet, and most of the green, are absent, leaving a light of yellowish colour. To traverse eight atmospheres the light has only to come from a point some eight degrees above the horizon. When the sun is near the horizon, it sends its rays not only to us and over us, but in every direction; and an eye placed some few thousand feet above the earth would see the sun almost of its midday colour, for sunset colours of the gorgeous character that we see at sea-level are almost absent at high altitudes. If a cloud or mist were at such an altitude the sunlight would strike it, and whilst only a small portion would be selectively scattered, owing to the general grossness of the particles, the major part would be reflected back to our eyes, and come from an altitude of over eight to ten degrees, and would therefore, after traversing the intervening atmosphere, reach us as the orange-coloured light of which we have just spoken. The clouds which are orange when near the sun, are usually higher than those which are simultaneously red or purple. The pea-green colour of the sky is often due to contrast, for the contrast colour to red is green, and this would make the blue of the sky appear decidedly greener. Sometimes, however, it is due to an absolute mixture of the blue of the sky and the orange light which illuminates the same haze. In the high Alps it is no uncommon occurrence for the snow-clad mountains to be tipped with the same crimson we have described as colouring the clouds, and this is usually just after sunset, when the sun has sunk so low beneath the horizon that the light has to traverse a greater thickness of dense air, and consequently to pass through a larger number of small particles than it has when just above the horizon. In this case the red of the sunlight mixes with blue light of the sky, and gives us the crimson tints. The deeper and richer tints of the clouds just after sunset are also due to the same cause, the thickness of air traversed being greater.

It is worth while to pause a moment and think what extraordinary sensual pleasure the presence of the small scattering particles floating in the air causes us; that without them the colouring which impresses itself upon us so strongly would have been a blank, and that artists would have to rely upon form principally to convey their feelings of art. Indeed without these particles there would probably be no sky, and objects would appear of the same hard definition as do the mountains in the atmosphereless moon. They would be only directly illuminated by sunlight, and their shadows by the light reflected from the surrounding bright surfaces.

CHAPTER VII.

Luminosity of the Spectrum to Normal-eyed and Colour-blind Persons—Method of determining the Luminosity of Pigments—Addition of one Luminosity to another.

The determination of the luminosity of a coloured object, as compared with a colourless surface illuminated by the same light, is the determination of the second colour constant. We will first take the pure spectrum colours, and show how their luminosity or relative brightness can be determined. Viewing a spectrum on the screen, there is not much doubt that in the yellow there is the greatest brightness, and that the brightness diminishes both towards the violet and red. Towards the latter the luminosity gradient is evidently more rapid than towards the former. This being the case, it is evident that, except at the brightest part there are always two rays, one on each side of the yellow, which must be equally luminous. If the spectrum be recombined to form a white patch upon the screen, and the slide with the slit be passed through it, patches of equal area of the different colours will successively appear; but the yellow patch will be the brightest patch. If the patch formed by the reflected beam be superposed over the colour patch, and the rod be interposed, we get a coloured stripe alongside a white stripe, and by placing our rotating sectors in the path of the reflected beam, the brightness of the latter can be diminished at pleasure. Suppose the sectors be set at 45°, which will diminish the reflected beam to one-quarter of its normal intensity, we shall find some place in the spectrum, between the yellow and the red, where the white stripe is evidently less bright than the coloured stripe, and by a slight shift towards the yellow, another place will be found where it is more bright. Between these two points there must be some place where the brightness to the eye is the same. This can be very readily found by moving the slit rapidly backwards and forwards between these two places of "too dark" and "too light," and by making the path the slit has to travel less and less, a spot is finally arrived at which gives equal luminosities. The position that the slit occupies is noted on the scale behind the slide, as is also the opening of the sectors, in this case 45°. As there is another position in the spectrum between the yellow and the violet, which is of the same intensity, this must be found in the same manner, and be similarly noted. In the same way the luminosities of colours in the spectrum, equivalent to the white light passing through other apertures of sectors, can be found, and the results may then be plotted in the form of a curve. This is done by making the scale of the spectrum the base of the curve, and setting up at each position the measure of the angular aperture of the sector which was used to give the equal luminosity or brightness to the white. By joining the ends of these ordinates by lines a curve is formed, which represents graphically the luminosity of the spectrum to the observer. In Fig. 11 the maximum luminosity was taken as 100, and the other ordinates reduced to that scale. The outside curve of the figure was plotted from observations made by the writer, who has colour vision which may be considered to be normal, as it coincides with observations made by the majority of persons. The inner curve requires a little explanation, though it will be better understood when the theory of colour vision has been touched upon.

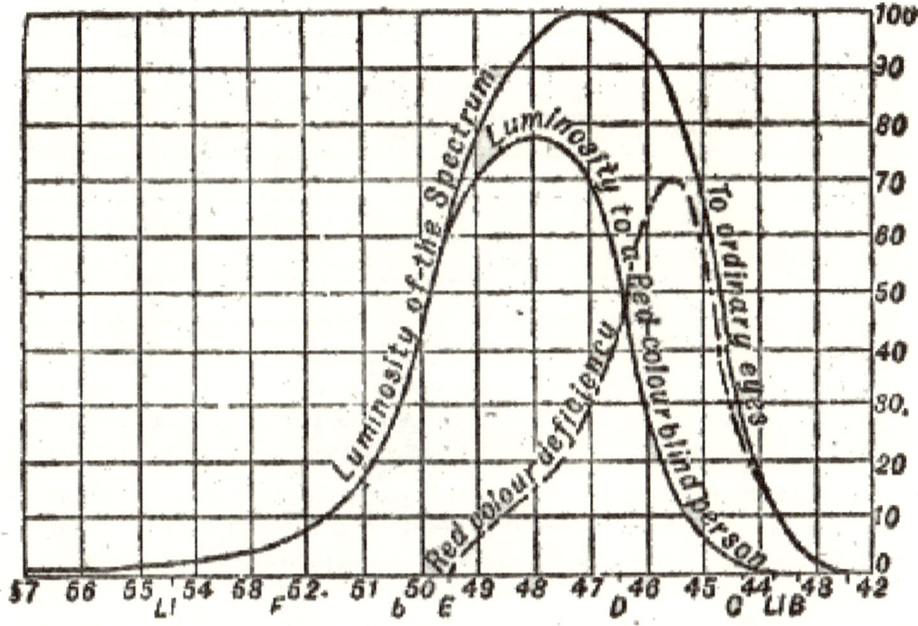

FIG. 11.

Luminosity Curve of the Spectrum of the Positive Pole of the Electric Light.

The observer in this case was colour-blind to the red, that is, he had no perception of red objects as red, but only distinguished them by the other colours which were mixed with the red. This being premised, we should naturally expect that his perception of the spectrum would be shortened, and this the observations fully prove. If it happened that his perceptions of all other colours were equally acute with a normal-eyed person, then his illumination value of the part of the spectrum occupied by the violet and green ought to be the same as that of the latter. The diagram shows that it is so, and the amount of red present in each colour to the normal-eyed observer is shown by the deficiency curve, which was obtained by subtracting the ordinates of colour-blind curve from those of the normal curve. There are other persons who are defective in the perception of green, and they again give a different luminosity curve for the spectrum. These variations in the perception of the luminosity of the different colours are very interesting from a physiological point of view, and this mode of measuring is a very good test as to defective colour vision. We shall allude to the subject of colour-blindness in a subsequent chapter.

The following are the luminosities for the colours fixed by the principal lines of the solar spectrum, and for the red and blue lines of lithium, to which reference has already been made.

Line.	Colour.	Luminosity.	
		Normal Eye.	Red Colour Blind.
A	Very dark Red	—	—
B	Red (Crimson)	1·0	0
Red Lithium	Red (Crimson)	8·5	·5
C	Red (Scarlet)	20·6	2·1
D	Orange	98·5	53·0
E	Green	50·0	49·0
F	Blue Green	7·0	7·0
Blue Lithium	Blue	1·9	1·9
G	Violet	·6	·6
H	Faint Lavender	—	—

The failure of the red colour-blind person to perceive red is very well shown from this table. It will for instance be noticed that he perceives about one-tenth of the light at C which the normal-eyed person perceives.

A modification of this plan can be employed for measuring the luminosity of the spectrum, and it is *excessively* useful, because we can adapt it to the measurement of colours other than these simple ones. In the plan already explained it was the colour in the patch that was altered, to get an equal luminosity with a certain luminosity of white light. In the modified plan the luminosity of the white light is altered, for the luminosity of the shadow illuminated by the reflected beam can be altered rapidly at will by opening or closing the apertures of the sectors whilst it is rotating. The slit in the slide is placed in the spectrum at any desired point, and the aperture of the sectors altered till equal luminosities are secured. The readings by this plan are very accurate, and give the same results as obtained by the previous method employed.

It must be remembered that we have so far dealt with colours which are spectrum colours, and which are intense because they are colours produced by the spectrum of an intensely bright source of light. By an artifice we can deduce from this curve the luminosity curve of the spectrum of any other source of light. If by any means we can compare, *inter se*, the intensity of the same rays in two different sources of light, one being the electric light, we can evidently from the above figure deduce the luminosity curve of the spectrum of the other source of light (see p. 109).

We can now show how we can adapt the last method to the measurement of the luminosity of the light reflected from pigments.

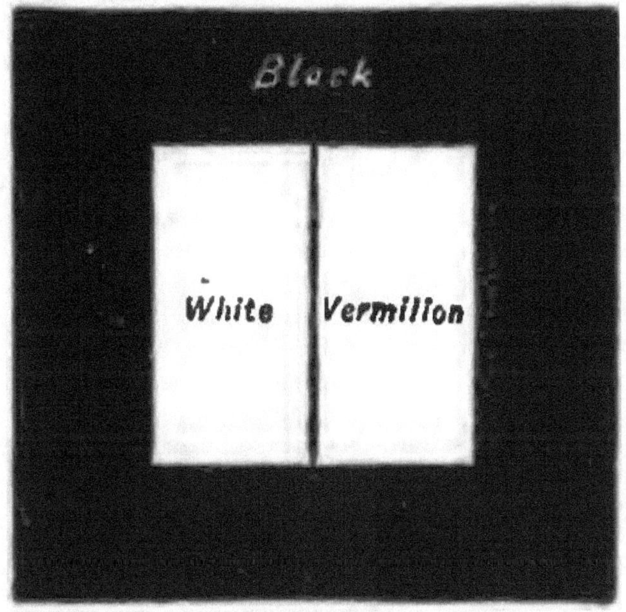

FIG. 12.
Rectangles of White and Vermilion.

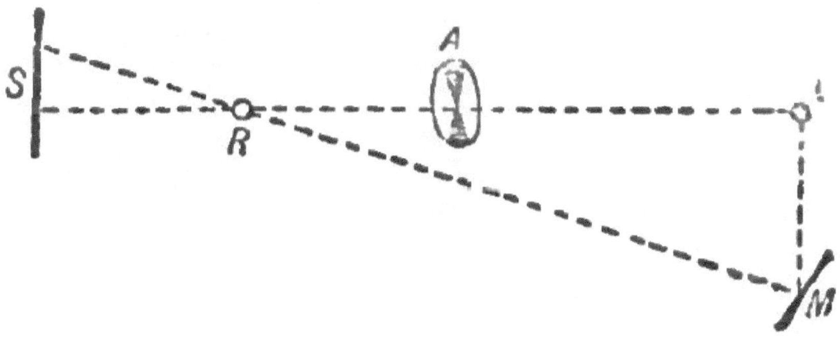

FIG. 13.
Arrangement for measuring the Luminosities of Pigments.

Suppose the luminosity of a vermilion-coloured surface had to be compared with a white surface when both were illuminated, say by gaslight, the following procedure is adopted. A rectangular space is cut out of black paper (Fig. 12) of a size such that its side is rather less than twice the breadth of the rod used to cast a shadow: a convenient size is about one inch broad by three-quarters of an inch in height. One-half of the aperture is filled with a white surface, and the other half with the vermilion-coloured surface. The light L (Fig. 13) illuminates the whole, and the rod R, a little over half an inch in breadth, is placed in such a position that it casts a shadow on the white surface, the edge of the shadow being placed accurately at the junction of the vermilion and white surface. A flat silvered mirror M is placed at such a distance and at such an angle that the light it reflects casts a second shadow on the vermilion surface. Between R and L are placed the rotating sectors A. The white strip is caused to be evidently too dark and then too light by altering the aperture of the sectors, and an oscillation of diminishing extent is rapidly made till the two shadows appear equally luminous. A white screen is next substituted for the vermilion and again a comparison made. The mean of the two sets of readings of angular apertures gives the relative value of the two luminosities. It must be stated, however, that any diffused light which might be in the room would relatively illuminate the white surface more than the coloured one. To obviate this the receiving screen is placed in a box, in the front of which a narrow aperture is cut just wide enough to allow the two beams to reach the screen. An aperture is also cut at the front angle of the box, through which the observer can see the screen. When this apparatus is adopted, its efficiency is seen from the fact that when the apertures of the rotating sectors are closed the shadow on the white surface appears quite black, which it would not have done had there been diffused light in any measurable quantity present within the box. The box, it may be stated, is blackened inside, and is used in a darkened room. The mirror arrangement is useful, as any variation in the direct light also shows itself in the reflected light. Instead of gaslight, reflected skylight or sunlight can be employed by very obvious artifices, in some cases a gaslight taking the place of the reflected beam. When we wish to measure luminosities in our standard light, viz. the light emitted from the crater of the positive pole of the arc-light, all we have to do is to place the pigment in the white patch of the recombined spectrum, and illuminate the white surface by the reflected beam, using of course the rod to cast shadows, as just described. The rotating sectors must be placed in either one beam or the other, according to the luminosity of the pigment.

The luminosities of the following colours were taken by the above method, and subsequently we shall have to use their values.

ELECTRIC LIGHT.

White	100
Vermilion	36
Emerald Green	30
Ultramarine	4·4
Orange	39·1
Black	4
Black (different surface)	5·1

Suppose we have two or more colours of the spectrum whose luminosities have been found, the question immediately arises, as to whether, when these two colours are combined, the luminosity of the compound colour is the sum of the luminosities of each separately. Thus suppose we have a slide with two slits placed in the spectrum, and form a colour patch of the mixture of the two colours and measure its luminosity, and then measure the luminosity of the patch first when one slit is covered up, and then the other. Will the sum of the two latter luminosities be equal to the measure of the luminosity of the compounded colour patch? One would naturally assume that it would, but the physicist is bound not to make any assumptions which are not capable of proof; and the truth or otherwise is perfectly easy to ascertain, by employing the method of measurement last indicated. Let us get our answer from such an experiment.

Colours Measured.	Observed Luminosity.
R	203·0
G	38·5
V	8·5
(R + G)	242
(G + V)	45
(R + V)	214
(R + G + V)	250

Three apertures were employed, one in the red, another in the green, and the third in the violet, and the luminosity was taken of each separately, next two together, and then all three combined, with the results given above.

The accuracy of the measurements will perhaps be best shown by adding the single colours together, the pairs and the single colours, and comparing these values with that obtained when the three colours were combined. When the pairs are shown they will be placed in brackets; thus (R + G) means that the luminosity of the compound colour made by red and green are being considered.

$$R + G + V \quad = \quad 250{\cdot}0$$
$$(R + G) + V \quad = \quad 250{\cdot}5$$
$$(R + V) + G \quad = \quad 252{\cdot}5$$
$$(G + V) + R \quad = \quad 248{\cdot}0$$
$$(R + G + V) \quad = \quad 250{\cdot}0$$

The mean of the first four is 250·25, which is only 1/10% different from the value of 250 obtained from the measurement of (R + G + V) combined. Other measures fully bore out the fact that the luminosity of the mixed light is equal to the sum of the luminosities of its components. It is true that we have here only been dealing with spectrum colours, but we shall see when we come to deal with the mixture of colours reflected from pigments that the same law is universally true.

It will be proved by and by that a mixture of three colours, and sometimes of only two colours, be they of the spectrum or of pigments, can produce the impression of white light. If then we measure all the components but one, and also the white light produced by all, then the luminosity of the remaining component can be obtained by deducting the first measures from the last. For instance, red, green and violet were mixed to form white light. The luminosity of the white being taken as 100, the red and violet were measured and found to have a luminosity of 44·5 and 3 respectively. This should give the green as having a luminosity of 52·5. The green was measured and found to be 53, whilst a measurement of the red and green together gave a luminosity of 96·5 instead of 97.

CHAPTER VIII.

Methods of Measuring the Intensity of the Different Colours of the Spectrum, reflected from Pigmented Surfaces—Templates for the Spectrum.

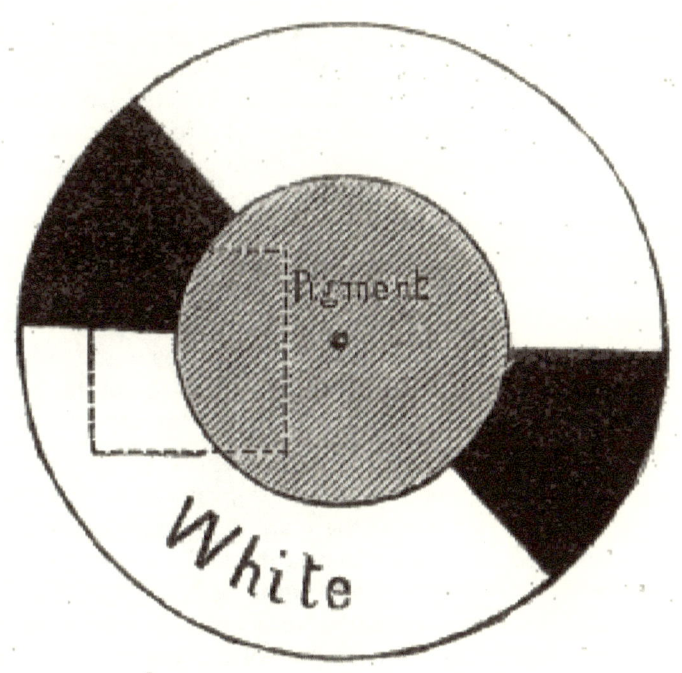

FIG. 14.
Measurement of the Intensity of Rays reflected from white and coloured surfaces.

We will now proceed to demonstrate how we can measure the amount of spectral light reflected by different pigments. Let us take a strip of card painted with a paste of vermilion, leaving half the breadth white; and similarly one with emerald green. If we place the first in the spectrum so that half its breadth falls on the red, and the other half on the white card, we shall see that apparently the red and orange rays are undiminished in intensity by reflection from the vermilion, but that in the green and beyond but very little of the spectrum is reflected. With the emerald green placed similarly in the spectrum, the red rays will be found to be absorbed, but in the green rays the full intensity of colour is found, fading off in the blue. What we now have to do is to find a method of comparing the intensities of the different rays reflected from the pigments, with those from the white surface. We will commence with the second of the two methods which the writer devised with this object, and then describe the first, which is more complex. Suppose we have, say a card disc three inches in diameter, painted with the pigment whose reflective power has to be measured, and place it on a rotating apparatus with black and white sectors of say five inches diameter, and capable of overlapping so as to show different proportions of black to white (see Fig. 42). If we throw a colour patch (shown in Fig. 14 as the area inside the dotted square) on the combination of black and white, and at the same time on the pigmented disc, it is probable that either one or other will be the brighter. By moving the slit along the spectrum it is evident, however, that a colour can be found which is equally reflected from them both whilst rotating. Take as an example the sectors as set at two parts white, to one part black, the centre disc being vermilion, the slit is moved along the spectrum until such a point is reached that the colour reflected from the ring and the disc appears of the same brightness, for it must be recollected that they cannot differ in hue, as the light is monochromatic. It will be found that the place where they match in brightness is in the red, the exact position being fixed by the scale at the back of the slide. Taking the proportion of black to white as three to one, the match will be found to take place in the orange. Increasing the proportion of black more and more, a point will be reached where the reflection takes place uniformly along the blue end of the spectrum, this will be from the green to the end of the violet. By sufficiently increasing the number of matches made, a curve of reflection can be made showing the exact proportion of each ray of the spectrum that is reflected. The uniform reflection along the blue end of the spectrum shows that a certain amount of white light is reflected from the pigment.

Next taking the emerald green disc, if we adopt the same procedure it will be found that for some shades of the ring there are two places in the spectrum from which the colours reflected give the same brightness. By plotting curves in exactly the same way as that shown for the curve of luminosity at page 78, substituting for the open aperture of the sector the angular value of the white used, we can show graphically the correct reflection for each part of the spectrum. Sometimes three places in the spectrum will be read, as giving equal reflections from the coloured disc and the grey ring.

The accompanying figures show the results obtained for reflection from vermilion, emerald green, and French blue, after having made a correction for the white by adding the amount which the black reflects.

The scale is that of the prismatic spectrum employed. On page 46 we stated that a white surface could be made to appear darker than a black surface, by illuminating the latter and cutting off the light from the former. By placing the black surface in place of one of the coloured ones, as shown in page 82, the luminosity of the black surface can be ascertained. In this case it was found that almost exactly 5% of the white light from the crater of the positive pole was reflected.In the table the original measures are shown, and also the corrected measures, and for convenience sake the intensity of every ray throughout the length of the spectrum reflected from white, has been taken as 100. The position of the reference lines on the scale (Fig. 15) are as follows—

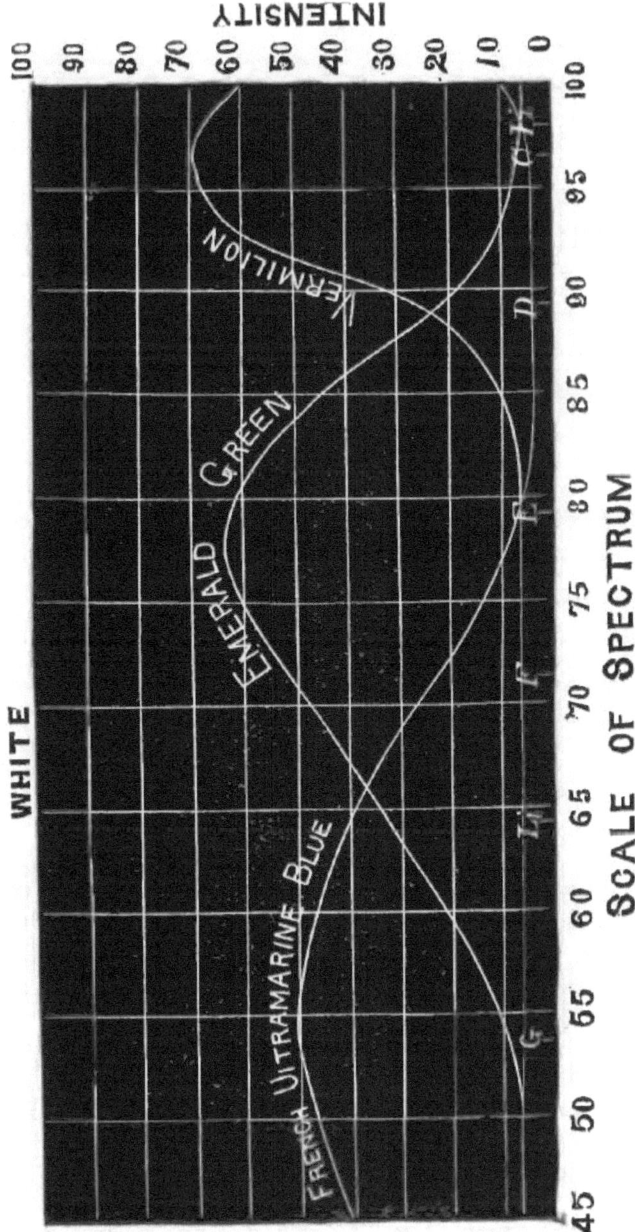

FIG. 15
Intensity of Rays reflected from Vermilion, Emerald Green, and French Ultramarine.

B=101, C=96·25, D=89, E=79·9, F=71·5, G=53·5.

VERMILION.

| White Sectors. | | | | Reading of Spectrum Scale. |
| Original Setting. | | White Corrected For Black. | Corrected White 100. | |
White.	Black.			
10	350	27·5	7·65	71½
20	340	37·0	10·15	84
30	330	46·5	12·95	86·2
50	310	65·5	18·10	88·0
70	290	84·5	23·50	88·7
90	270	103·5	29·7	89·5
120	240	132·0	37·2	90·3
150	210	160·5	45·0	91
180	180	189·0	52·5	91·6
210	150	217·5	60·2	92·5
220	140	227·0	63·2	93·5
230	130	236·5	66·2	94·5
240	120	246·0	68·5	96
230	130	236·5	66·2	97·7
210	150	217·5	60·2	100·0

EMERALD GREEN.

| White Sectors. | | | | Reading of Spectrum Scale. |
| Original Setting. | | White Corrected For Black. | Corrected White 100. | |
White.	Black.			
10	350	27·5	7·65	50
20	340	37·0	10·15	54
30	330	46·5	12·95	55
50	310	65·5	18·10	57·5
70	290	84·5	23·5	60·0
90	270	103·5	29·7	63·5
110	250	122·5	34·7	65·5
130	230	141·5	39·5	67·5
150	210	160·5	45·0	68·5

170	190	179·5	50·0	71
190	170	195·5	54·7	73·5
210	150	217·5	60·2	75·0
220	140	227	63·2	76
220	140	227	63·2	78
210	150	217·5	60·2	80
190	170	198·5	54·7	82
170	190	179·5	50·0	83
150	210	160·5	45·0	84
130	230	141·5	39·5	85
110	250	122·5	34·7	86·5
90	270	103·5	29·7	87·5
70	290	84·5	23·5	88·5
50	310	65·5	18·10	90·0
30	330	46·5	12·95	92
20	340	37·0	10·15	94
10	350	27·5	7·65	98

FRENCH ULTRAMARINE BLUE.

WHITE SECTORS.				READING OF SPECTRUM SCALE.
ORIGINAL SETTING.		WHITE CORRECTED FOR BLACK.	CORRECTED WHITE 100.	
WHITE.	BLACK.			
0	360	18·0	5·0	84
10	350	27·5	7·65	80
20	340	37·0	10·15	77
30	330	46·5	12·95	75
40	320	56·0	15·6	74
60	300	75·0	20·7	72·5
80	280	94·0	25·5	70·5
100	260	113·0	32·5	68
120	240	132·0	37·2	66·5
140	220	151·0	42·3	62·5
160	200	170·0	47·4	59·5
170	190	179·5	50·0	55
160	200	170·0	47·4	51

140	220	151·0	42·3	46
0	360	18·0	5·0	95
10	350	27·5	7·65	98
20	340	37·0	10·15	99
30	330	46·5	12·95	110

These three measurements have been given in full, since they will be useful for reference when other experiments are described.

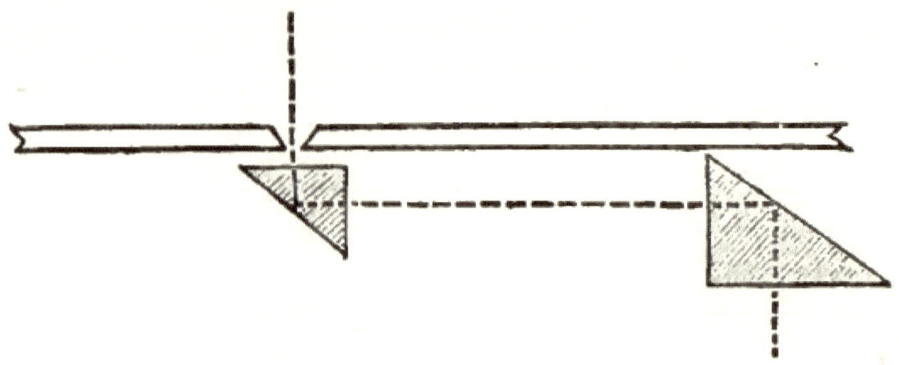

FIG. 16.
Method of obtaining two Patches of identical Colour.

When we have to measure the colour transmitted through coloured bodies, we have to adopt a slightly different plan, which is extremely accurate. The first thing necessary is to make some arrangement whereby two beams of identical colour—that is, of the same wave-length—reach the screen, one of which passes through the transparent body to be measured, and the other unabsorbed. If we in addition have some means of equalizing the intensity of the two beams, we can then tell the amount cut off by the body through which one beam passes. The method that would be first thought of would be to use two spectra, from two sources of light; but should we adopt that plan there would be no guarantee that the spectra would not vary in intensity from time to time. The point then that had to be aimed at was to form two spectra from the same source of light, and with the same beam that passes through the slit of the collimator. Here we are helped by the property of Iceland spar, which is able to split up a ray into two divergent rays. By placing what is called a double-image prism of Iceland spar at the end of the collimator, we get two divergent beams of light falling on the prisms, and by turning the double-image prism we are able to obtain two spectra on the screen of the camera one above the other, and if the slit of the slide be sufficiently long two beams would issue through it of identical colour, and separated from one another by a dark space, the breadth of which depends on the length of the slit of the collimator. It is to be observed that by this arrangement we have exactly what we require: a light from one source passes through the same slit, is decomposed by the same prisms, and as the beams diverge in a plane passing through the slit of the collimator, the length of spectrum is the same. The problem to solve is how to utilize these two spectra now we have got them. We can make the light from the top spectrum pass through the coloured body by the following artifice. Let us place a right-angled prism in front of the top slit, reflecting say the beam to the right, and after it has travelled a certain distance, catch it by another right-angled prism, and thus reflect it on to the screen. Already in the path of the ray, issuing through the slit from the bottom spectrum, the lens L_4 is placed, forming a square patch on the screen. By placing a similar lens in the path of the other ray after reflection from the second right-angled prism, we can superpose a second patch of the same colour over the first patch, and by putting a rod in the path of the two beams we can have as before two shadows side by side, but this time each illuminated by the same colour. One shadow will be more strongly illuminated than the other, owing to the different intensities of beams into which the double-image prism splits up the primary ray. The two, however, can be equalized by placing a rotating apparatus in the path of one of the beams. When equalized the sector is read off, and tells us how much brighter one spectrum is than the other. Thus suppose in the direct beam the sectors had to be closed to an angle of 80°, to effect this, the bottom spectrum would be 180/80, or 2·25 times brighter than the bottom spectrum. It should be noted that as the two spectra are formed by the identical quality of light, this same ratio will hold good throughout their length. If it does not, it shows that the double-image prism is not in adjustment, and that the same rays are not coming through the slit in the slide, and it must be rotated till the readings throughout are the same. One of the most sensitive tests for adjustment is to form a patch with orange light, when the slightest deviation from adjustment will be seen by the two patches differing in hue.

We can now place the coloured transparent object in the path of the beam which is most convenient, and by again equalizing the shadows, measure the amount it cuts off; this we can do for any ray we choose. As both right-angled prisms can be attached to the card or slide which moves across the spectrum, nothing besides the card need be moved. In the following diagram we have the proportion of rays transmitted by the three different glasses, red, green, and blue, in terms of the unabsorbed spectrum. Take for instance on the scale of the spectrum the number 11. The curve shows that at that particular part of the spectrum which lies in the blue, the blue glass only allowed 4/100 or 1/25 of the ray to pass, whilst the green glass allowed 10/100 or 1/10 to pass. So at scale No. 4 in the orange, through the blue only 2% was transmitted, through the green glass 4%, and through the red 20%.

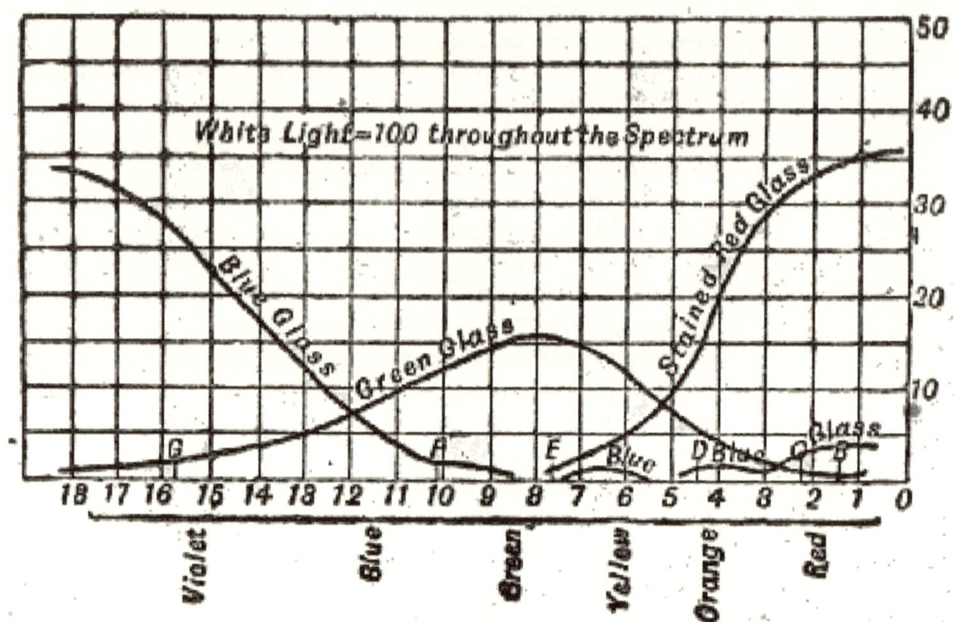

FIG. 17.
Absorption by Red, Blue, and Green Glasses.

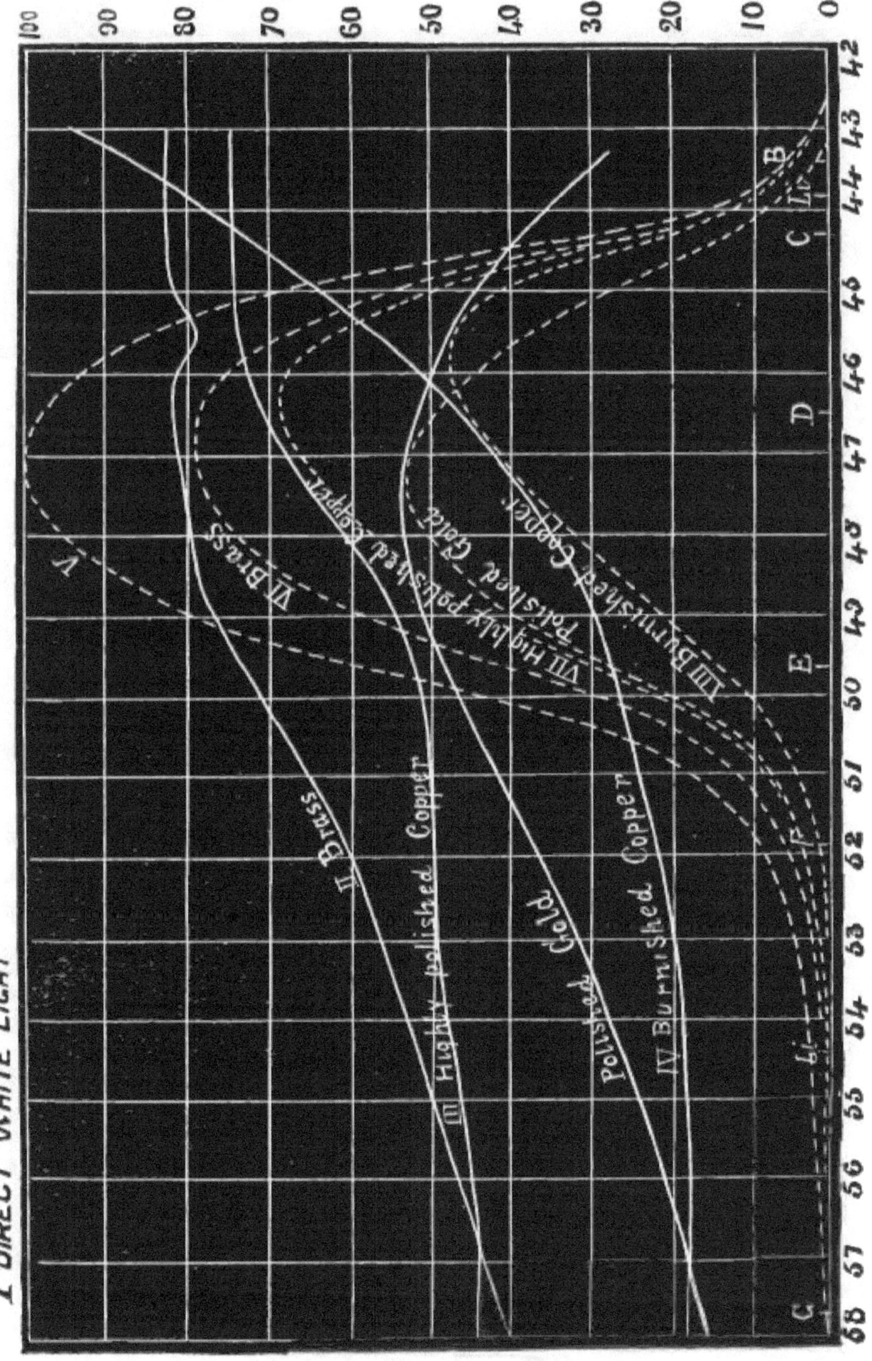

FIG. 18.
Light reflected from Metallic Surfaces.

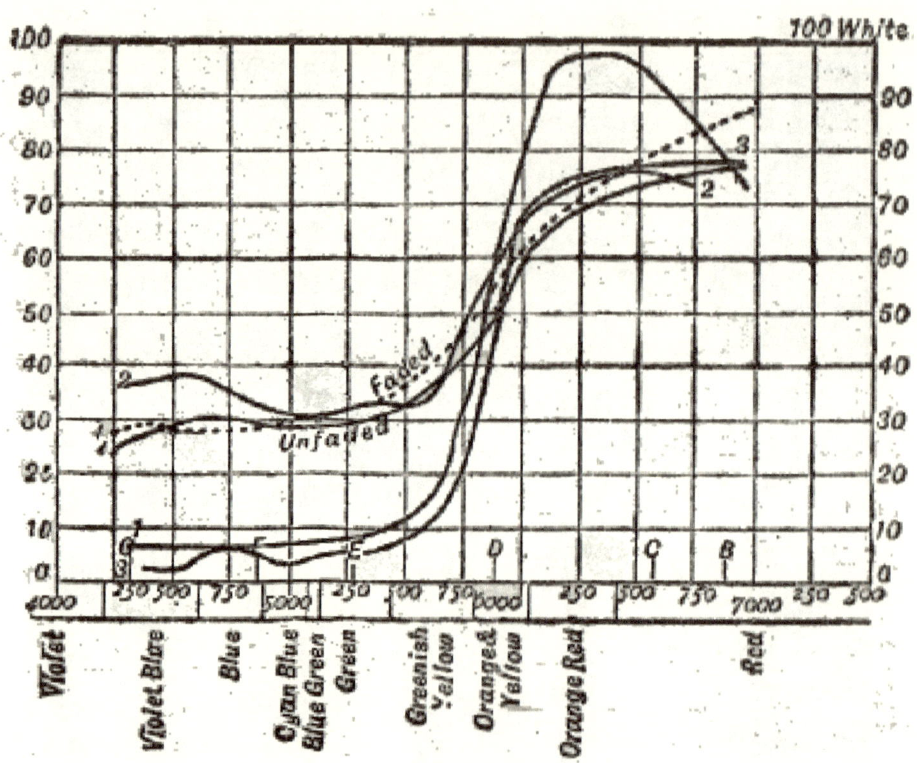

FIG. 19.

1. Vermilion 2. Carmine. 3. Mercuric Iodide. 4. Indian Red.

From such curves as these we can readily derive the luminosity curves of the spectrum, after the white light has passed through the coloured object. All we have to do is to alter the ordinates of the luminosity curve of white light in the proportion to the intensities of the rays before and after passing through the object. It will be seen that when the luminosity curve of the spectrum of *any* source is known, this method holds good.

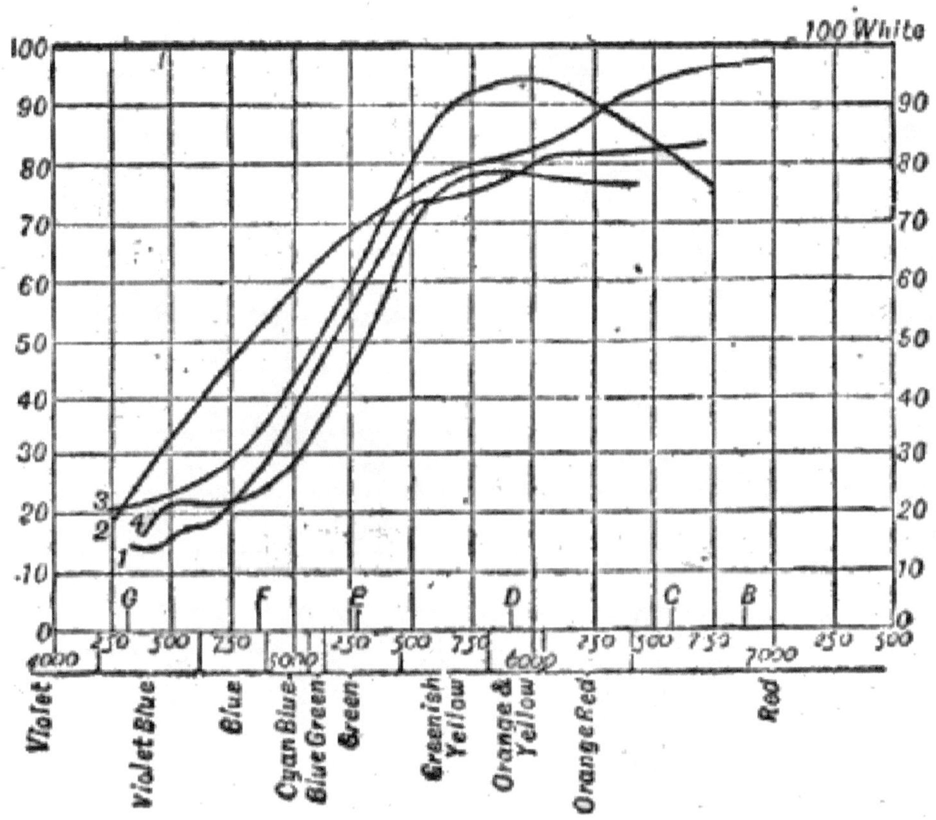

FIG. 20.

1. Gamboge. 2. Indian Yellow. 3. Cadmium Yellow. 4. Yellow Ochre.

The intensity of the different rays of the spectrum reflected from metallic surfaces can also be measured, if for the first or second right-angled prism a small piece of the metal is substituted, using it as a reflecting surface, as can also the rays reflected from any surface which is bright and polished. In Fig. 18 the dotted curves show the *luminosity* of the spectrum reflected from the different metals, curve V being that of white light. These curves are derived by reducing the ordinates of curve V proportionately to the intensity curves. Thus at 49 brass reflects 77% of the light, and the luminosity of the white is 80. The luminosity of the light from the brass is therefore 77/100 of 80, or 61. This shows the method which is adopted, of deducing luminosities from intensities.

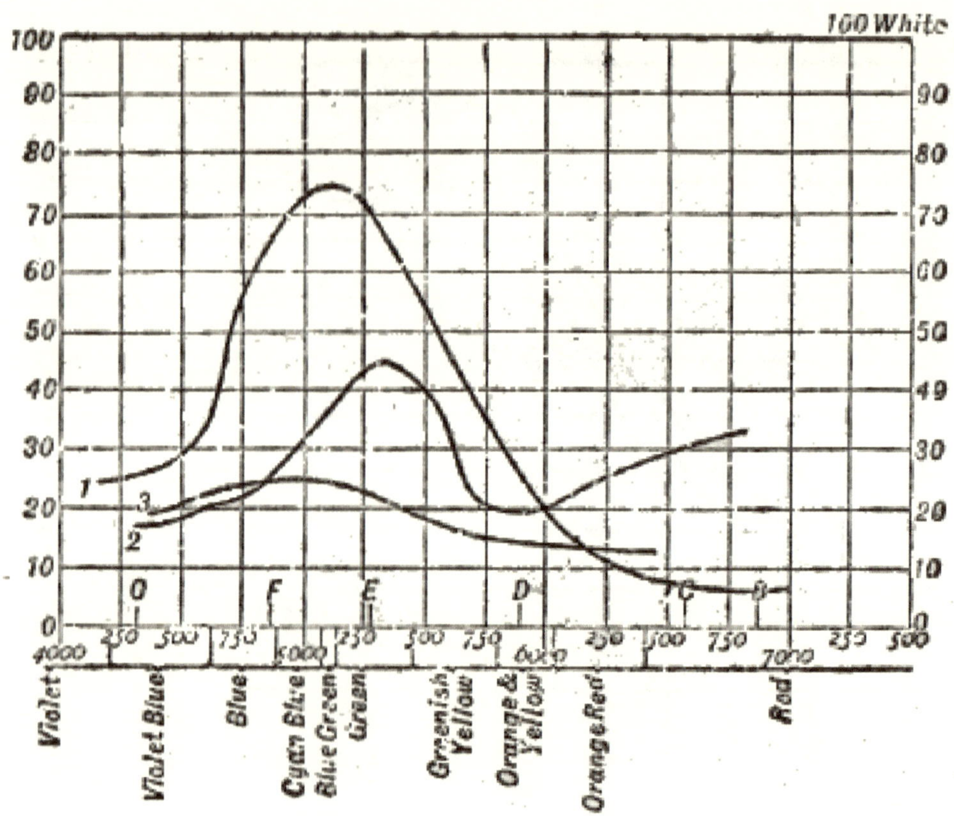

FIG. 21.
1. Emerald Green. 2. Chromous Oxide. 3. Terre Verte.

The light reflected from pigments can also be measured by the same plan. The procedure adopted is that carried out when measuring their luminosities, viz. to cause the ray from one spectrum to fall on a strip of a white surface, and that from the other on a strip of the coloured surface (see page 82). This is a more convenient method than that just described, when the coloured surface is small. The annexed figures (Figs. 19, 20, 21, 22) show the results obtained from various pigments.

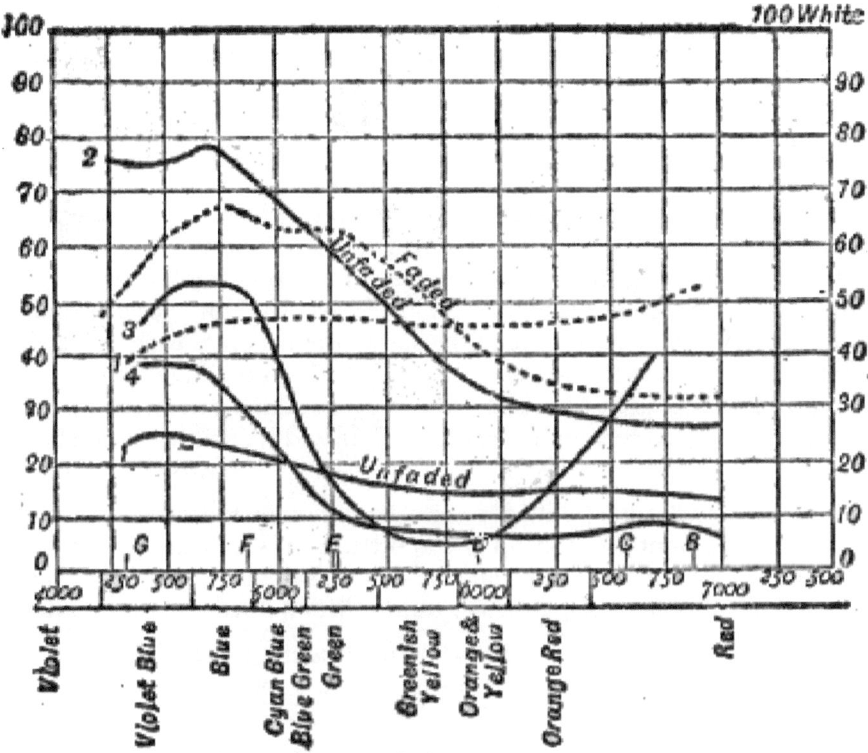

FIG. 22.

1. Indigo. 2. Antwerp Blue. 3. Cobalt. 4. French Ultramarine.

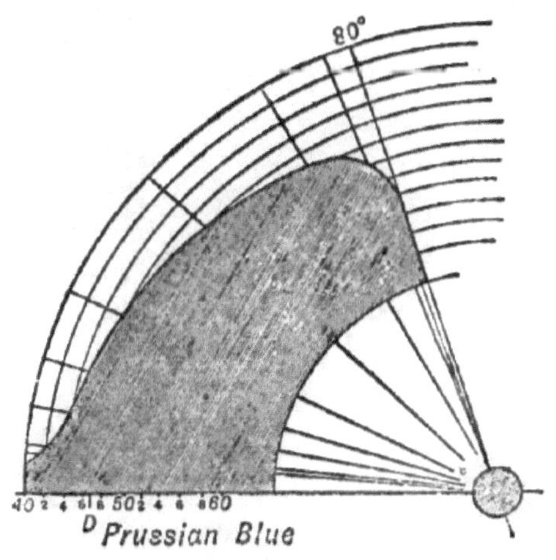

FIG. 23.

Method of obtaining a Colour Template.

From curves such as these we are able to produce the colour of the pigment on the screen from the spectrum itself. This is a useful proof of the truth of the measurements made. To do this we must mark off on a card (Fig. 23) the absolute scale of the spectrum along the radius of a circle, and draw circles at the various points of the scale from its centre. From the same centre we must draw lines at angles to the fixed radius corresponding to the various apertures of the sectors required at the various points of the scale to measure the light reflected from a pigment. Where each radial line cuts the circle drawn through the particular point of the scale to which its angle has reference, gives us points which joined give a curved figure. Such a figure, when cut out and rotated in front of the spectrum in the proper position (as for instance by making the D sodium line correspond with that on the scale), will cut off exactly the same proportion of each colour that the pigment absorbs. The spectrum, when recombined, should give a patch of the exact colour of that measured. The spectrum must be made narrow, as the template is only theoretically correct for a spectrum of the width of a line, as can be readily seen.

Templates like these will always enable any colour to be reproduced on the screen, and if the light be used for the spectrum in which the colour has to be viewed, be it sunlight, gaslight, starlight—whatever light it is—the colour obtained will be that which the pigment would reflect if it were viewed in that light.

The identity of the colour produced on the screen by this plan with that measured, can be readily seen by placing the latter in the reflected beam of white light alongside the coloured patch formed on the white surface.

FIG. 24.
Template of Carmine.

In Fig. 24 we have a mask or template of carmine, which was used for determining if the measurements were right. The black fingerlike-looking space on the right was the amount of red reflected light, and the other that of the blue and violet; scarcely any light at all was reflected from the green part of the spectrum.

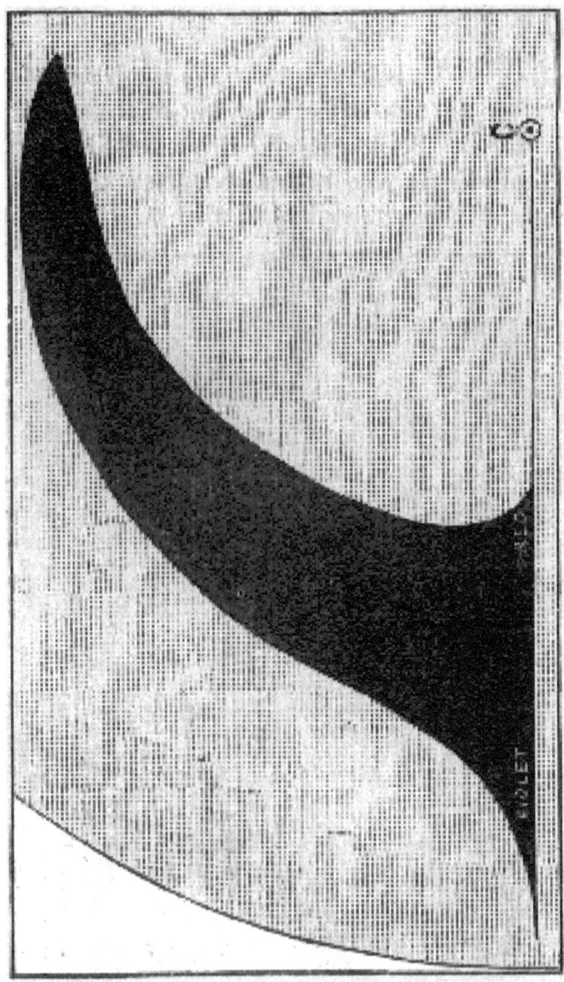

FIG. 25.
Template of Luminosity of White Light.

On page 108 we have given the diagram of the luminosity of the spectrum in reference to a standard white light. It will bring this luminosity more home if, in a similar manner to that described above, we make a template of this curve (Fig. 25). We can place a narrow slit horizontally in front of the condensing lens of the optical lantern, and throw an image of it on to the screen. If in close contact with this slit we rotate the template, we shall have on the screen a graduated strip of white light, giving in black and white the apparent luminosity of the spectrum as seen by the eye.

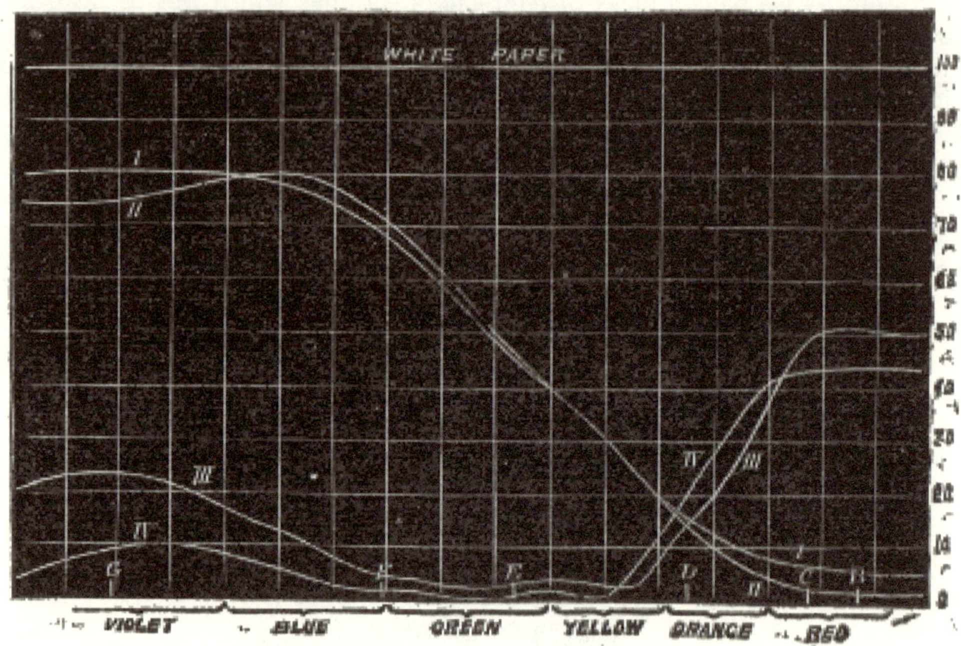

FIG. 26.
Absorption of transmitted and reflected Light by Prussian Blue and Carmine.

It has been stated in chapter V., that it is generally immaterial whether a pigment is in contact with the paper or away from it, so long as the light passes through the pigment. The above figure (Fig. 26) shows the truth of this assertion. I. and II. are the curves taken of the light transmitted by Prussian blue and carmine respectively, and III. and IV., from the light reflected from these colours on paper.

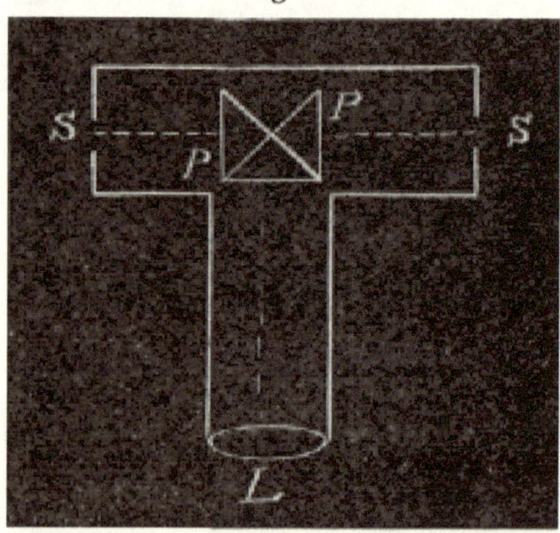

FIG. 27.
Collimator for comparing the intensity of two sources of Light.

To measure the difference in the intensities of the rays of different sources of light we can use a spectroscopic arrangement with two slits (S) (Fig. 27) placed in a line at right angles to the axis of the collimator. One slit is a little below the other, the rays being reflected to the collimating lens L, by means of two right-angled prisms P, and two spectra are formed, one above the other. By placing the rotating sectors in front of one of the sources, the intensities of the different parts of the spectrum can be equalized and measured.

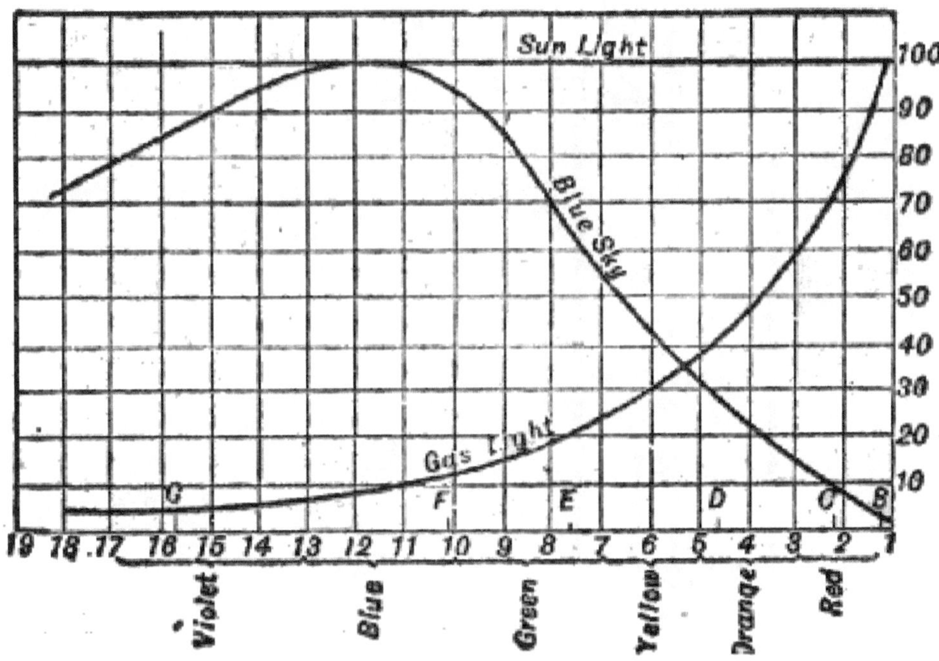

FIG. 28.
Spectrum Intensities of Sunlight, Gaslight, and Blue Sky.

The curves for the annexed figure (Fig. 28) were derived from measures taken in this manner. If the rays of a May-day sun are taken at 100, it will be seen what a rapid diminution there is in the green and the blue rays in gaslight. Gaslight only possesses about 20% of the green rays, whilst of the violet hardly 5%. On the other hand the light which comes to us from the sky shows a very marked falling off in the yellow and red rays. A very easy experiment will convince us of the difference in colour between skylight and gaslight. If we let a beam of daylight fall on a sheet of paper at the end of a blackened box, and cast a shadow with a rod by such a beam, and then bring a lighted candle or gas-flame so that it casts another shadow of the rod alongside, one shadow will be illuminated by the artificial light, and the other by the daylight. The difference in colour will be most marked: the blue of the latter light and the yellow of the former being intensified by the contrast (see page 198).

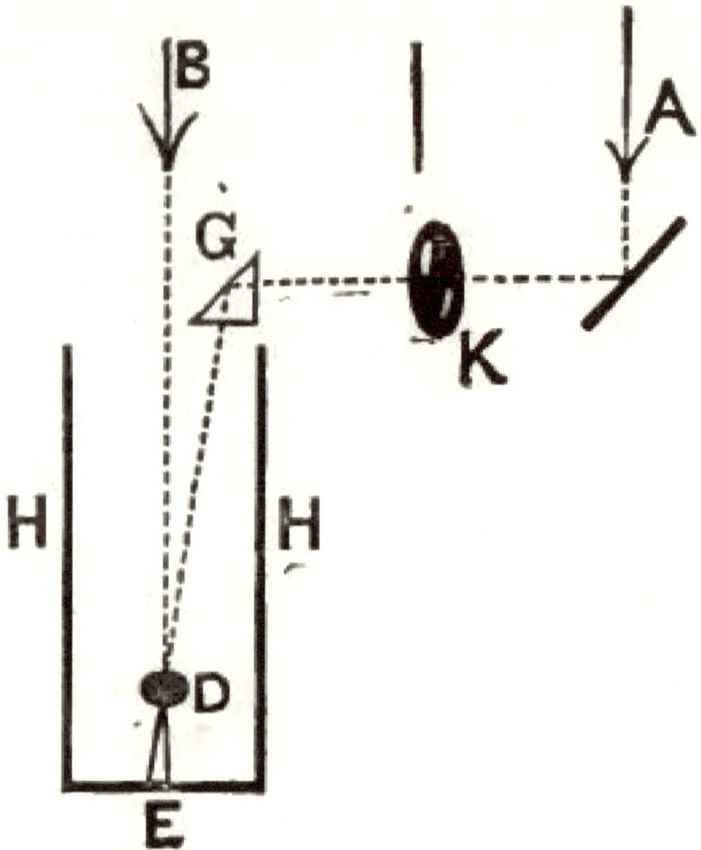

FIG. 29.
Comparison of Sun and Sky Lights.

By a little trouble the blue light from the sky may be compared with sunlight. A beam of light B (Fig. 29) is reflected by a silvered glass mirror from the blue sky into the box HH, at the end of which is a screen E. Another mirror A, which is preferably of plain glass, reflects light from the sun on to a second unsilvered mirror G (shown in the figure as a prism), which again reflects it on to the screen, and each of these lights casts a shadow from the rod D; K are rotating sectors to diminish the sunlight, and we can make two equally bright shadows alongside one another. The bluer colour of the sky will be very evident.

CHAPTER IX.

Colour Mixtures—Yellow Spot in the Eye—Comparison of Different
 Lights—Simple Colours by mixing Simple Colours—Yellow and
 Blue form White.

The colour of an object in nature, without exception we might almost say, is
due, not to one simple spectrum colour, or even to a mixture of two or three of
them, but to the whole of white light, from which bands of colour are more or less
abstracted, the absorption taking place over a considerable portion or portions of
the spectrum. Notwithstanding this we shall now experimentally show that every
colour can be formed by the simple admixture of not more than three simple colours, if they be rightly chosen, and from this we shall make a deduction regarding
vision itself. We are in a position to obtain three simple colours by means of a slide
containing three slits. Now for our purpose we require that the three slits can be
placed in any part of the spectrum, and that they can be narrowed or widened at
pleasure. Instead of a card the writer uses a metal slide, as shown in Fig. 30.

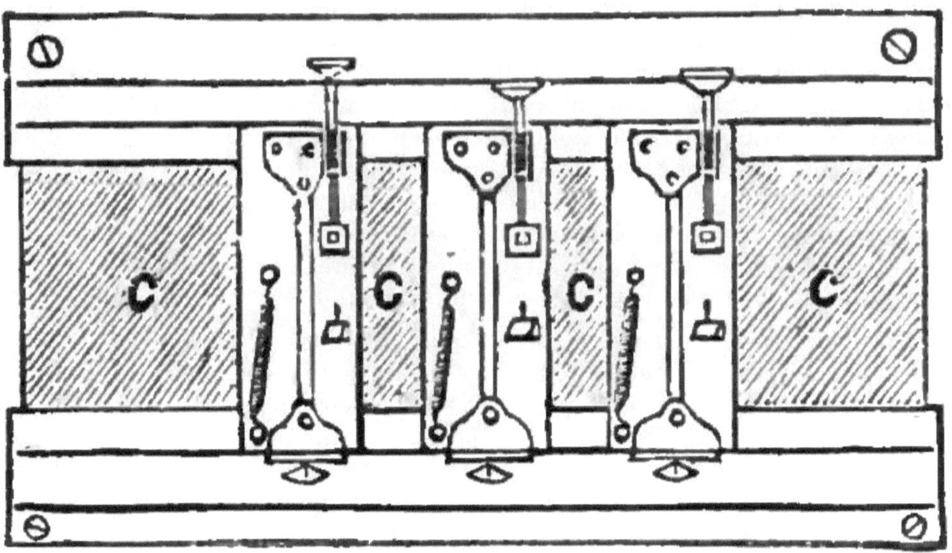

FIG. 30.
Slide with slits to be used in the Spectrum.

It will be seen that the three slits can be closed or opened from the centre by a parallel motion. They also slide in a couple of grooves, so that they can be moved along the frame into any position. The position they occupy is indicated by a scale engraved on the front of the slide. Behind the grooves in which the slits move are another pair of grooves, into which small pieces of card CCCC can slide, and thus close the apertures between the slits. By this arrangement all rays except those coming through the slits themselves are cut off. The metal frame fits on to an outer wooden frame, which slides in the grooves used with the card in the apparatus as already described. It is convenient always to keep the scale on the back of this wooden slide in the same position as regards the shadow of the needle-point used for registering the position, and to move the slits along their grooves when a change in position is required. Using these three slits three different colours can be thrown on the same square patch on the screen.

A very crucial experiment is to see if we can make white light by the admixture of three colours, for if this can be done it almost follows that any colour can be formed. We must use the colour patch apparatus, and begin with placing one slit in the violet near the line G, another between E and F, and a third between B and C of the solar spectrum, and fill up the gaps between them with cards as shown in the figure. For our present purpose it is better to make the colour patch and the white patch touch each other, not using the rod, as by this means we avoid fringes of colour. We shall find that the aperture of the slits can be so altered that we can produce a perfect match with the white reflected light. By placing the rotating sectors in front of the reflected beam we can reduce its intensity, so that the two patches are equally bright. By a tapering wedge we can measure the width of the slits, and thus get the proportions of these three different colours which must be used to give the white. This is a sample of the method that we employ when we match any other colour. Suppose, for instance, it be wished to measure the colour of a solution of bichromate of potash; it is placed in the path of the reflected light, and we have an orange strip of light which we have to match. In this case it will be found that the slit in the blue has to be closed entirely, and only the green and red slits opened. The intensities of the two lights are equalized by the rotating sectors as before. So again with a solution of permanganate of potash. In this instance no green light will be required (or if any of it but a trifle), and the colour of the permanganate will be formed by the rays coming through the blue and red slits.

This plan is a very useful one for measuring all kinds of transparent colours in terms of three rays. The method of finding the intensity of any ray of the spectrum transmitted by any such medium has already been explained. The latter has one advantage over the former, in that the measurements by it are exact, whatever source of light be used to form the spectrum. By the method now described this is not the case. For instance, the colour of permanganate of potash may be matched in the electric light with the red and blue slits. If the limelight were substituted for the electric light, it would be found that the slits would require other apertures, not proportional to those already formed, to match the colour of this substance.

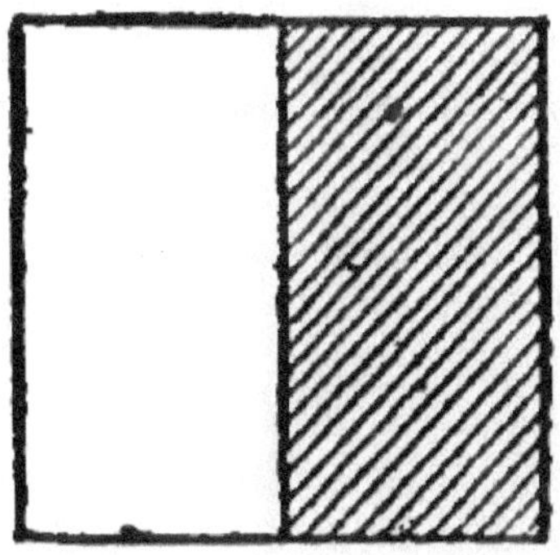

FIG. 31.
Screen on which to match Gamboge.

If we wish to register the tint of any pigment, we have to slightly alter our mode of procedure. Suppose, for instance, we wish to register the colour of gamboge. In such a case we paint a small bit of card (Fig. 31) with the pigment, and divide the white space on which the colour patches are thrown into two parts, and cover one-half with the pigmented card, leaving the other half white. The reflected beam illuminates the pigment, and the spectrum patch the white. The widths of the three slits are then altered till the two tints agree, and the brightness matched by means of the rotating sectors.

There are certain sad and æsthetic colours which it might be considered cannot be matched by a mixture of three colours. A brown colour, or "eau de nil," might appear to come out of the range of matching. These colours, however, can be matched in precisely the same manner as the brighter colours are matched. Thus a brown pigment will be found to require red and a little green, and a trifle of blue; and the only difference between it and a brighter shade of the same colour, is that more total light has to be cut off from it to give the sombreness. A sad colour only means a pigment or dye which reflects but little light, and if that be so it can naturally be matched by using but very small quantities of the compounding colours.

There is one curious phenomenon to which attention may be called in this matching, which is worthy of remark. The match will be found to differ according as the patches are compared from a distance of a couple of feet, or from a considerable distance. More green will be required in the latter case than in the former. If matched at a distance of about six feet, and the eyes be then turned so that the edge of the patch falls on their centres, it will be noticed that the colour mixture appears of a green hue. This last experiment indicates that the retina is not equally sensitive for all colours throughout its area. Physiologists tell us that what is known as the yellow spot occupies a central position in the retina, and that it absorbs a part of the spectrum lying in the green. Now when the eyes are close to the patch, its image occupies a considerable part of the retina, and the colour is compounded as it were of the colour as seen on the yellow spot, and of that beyond it, for the yellow spot will take in an image of from six to eight degrees in angular measurement. When viewed at a distance we have the image of the patch falling almost entirely on the yellow spot, and hence a greater quantity of green is required, as it has to make up the deficiency caused by the absorption. When the eyes are turned a little on one side the image falls on the outside of the yellow spot, and the patch illuminated by the mixed light appears green, compared with the patch illuminated with the white reflected beam.

It is thus evident that when colour matches have to be made, the distance of the eye from the screen should always be stated, as also the dimensions of the patches viewed. It may be fairly asked why, if the half patch illuminated by the mixed colours appears greener when the eye is turned, the other should not equally do so. This is a very fair question to ask. It must be remembered that one strip is illuminated with white light, in which every coloured ray of light is compounded, whilst in the other only three rays are blended. The green ray chosen happens to be taken from that part of the spectrum which is absorbed by the yellow spot; but all of the green rays of the spectrum are not so much absorbed, hence in ordinary white light, in which all the green rays are present, only a small percentage of the total green in the spectrum is absorbed, compared with that absorbed from the single green ray with which the match is made. No doubt both patches are really greener when the eye receives the impression of their images outside the yellow spot, but one is much greener than the other, and it is thus *comparatively* green. It is possible to make a match with some colours with a blue-green in which the phenomenon described does not appear; but in cases where a match has to be made with colours in which but little blue is required, it would be impossible to make it, owing to the blue existent in such a green-blue ray.

We will now return to our compounding of three colours to make white. Why have we chosen the positions of the slits which we did in the spectrum for its formation? Would not other positions answer as well? Let us give our answer by experiment. Let us move the slit which is now in the green towards the red; we shall find that as we do so — and keeping the blue slit of the same width — that we shall have to close the red slit, and alter the aperture of the green slit itself. If we reason on this point we shall be forced to the conclusion that the green slit lets through more red light of some description, as less red from the red slit is required to make the match. If we move the green slit almost into the yellowish green, we shall find that the red slit has to be entirely closed, and that white light is formed of the two colours, yellowish green and violet. This shows us that the yellowish green colour here used is formed by a mixture of the red and green rays which passed through the two slits in their original positions. If we replace the slits in these positions and close the violet slit, we are at once able to verify it.

If we again form white light with the slits in their original positions, and move the green slit towards the blue, we shall find that, keeping the red slit at a constant aperture, the blue slit will have to be closed, and the green slit altered in width. The necessity of lessening the aperture of the blue slit shows that there is a certain amount of blue light coming through the green slit. At one point, when the slit has travelled into the blue-green, the blue slit may be entirely closed, and white light be formed of this and the red, showing that the blue-green colour is composed of the same proportions of blue and green which passed through the blue and green slits in their original position. The positions chosen were arrived at by the writer from experiments made in this manner, moving first one slit and then the others, and the position of the green slit was confirmed by a consideration of the neutral point which exists in a green colour-blind person's spectrum.

The method of mixing three colours together gives us a means of imitating all kinds of white light, as it does of coloured light. At page 110 we have already given a diagram of the relative amounts of spectrum colours in sunlight, skylight and gaslight. If we by any means throw a patch of the light which we wish to match on the patch formed by the colour patch apparatus, and interpose the rod, we can measure the apertures of the three slits, and thus arrive at the relative proportions of each colour present. In an experiment carried out, sunlight, the electric arc-light, and gaslight were compared in this manner. The following are the results, the red being near the C line, the green near the E line, and the violet near the G line of the solar spectrum.

	SUNLIGHT.	ELECTRIC LIGHT.	GASLIGHT.	SKYLIGHT.
Red	100	100	100	100
Green	193	203	95	256
Violet	228	250	27	760

Now from the above it might seem that as three simple spectrum colours will give us the colour of any pigment, that therefore two colours ought to give us the same colour as any intermediate simple colours in the spectrum which lie between them; for instance, that the simple blue-green ought to be obtained by mixing spectral green and spectral violet together. This can be ascertained with a single colour patch apparatus, by cutting a slit in the card that fills up the aperture between the two adjustable slits, and deflecting the beam transmitted through it by a right-angled prism, and back on to the screen through another similar prism, as described in chapter VIII. It is more convenient, however, to use a duplicate apparatus precisely similar to the first, with the exception that no collimator is required, placing them side by side, and mirrors making the reflected beam from the first traverse the second set of prisms. There will be a reflected beam from the second apparatus, which can be utilized in the same way as was that from the first apparatus, and the two spectra will vary together in brightness, as will also the new reflected beam, since they all are formed by the light coming through one slit. A patch of the colour intermediate between the two is thrown on the screen from the second apparatus, and the second patch from the first apparatus overlaps it. A rod placed in the usual manner throws two shadows, which are illuminated by the two different beams. If blue-green be a colour it is wished to match, it will be found that no matter in what part of the violet and green the slits are placed, no match can be effected. But if some very small quantity of red light be mixed with simple blue-green, that then a colour identical in every respect as regards the eye can be obtained from the violet and green of the first apparatus. It must be remembered that a mixture of red, green and violet form white, and that they are mixed in definite proportions. No matter how feeble in intensity the white may be, the same proportions will still obtain. In the above experiment, as the blue-green must contain violet and green, the small quantity of red must combine with the proper proportion of violet and green, and will form white light, so that the match is obtained by the residues of the violet and green mixed with the small quantity of white light, of which the red is the indicator.

We can test the truth of this argument in a very simple way. If we add to the colour with which the match has to be made a small quantity of white light from the reflected beam, cutting off more or less by the rotating sectors, we can get the exact hue of the impure blue-green made by the mixture of the colours coming through the two slits; and further we shall find that the amount of white added corresponds with the amount of red which would be required when the components of the white light in the terms of the three colours are taken into account. For spectrum colours between the violet and the green it may therefore safely be said that no match can be effected by the mixture of violet and green light; but that it always gives the intermediate colour diluted with white light. For colours between the green and the red of the spectrum, a very close, if indeed not an exact match, can be made with the red and green slits, without the addition of white.

If we take from the second apparatus light from above the position of the violet slit in the first apparatus, that is, nearer the limit of visibility, it will be found that a match is made, for at all events a very considerable way with the violet slit alone, by merely reducing the aperture, thus showing that the colour is the same, only less intense. In the same way it will be seen that the rays coming from any point between the lower limit of the spectrum to a little below the C line are identical in colour.

As we have arrived at the fact that in colour mixtures of violet and green, white light is to be found in the colour produced, it follows that either the violet or the green, or both, must themselves contain some small proportion of white. It might perhaps be said that violet is really a mixture of red and blue, and hence the white in the mixture with the green; but if in the first apparatus we place one slit in the purest blue we can find, and the other in the red, and throw a violet patch on the screen from the second apparatus, we shall be unable to form the same hue of violet by any means; it will always be diluted with white. Now as the very blue we are using, if matched as above by green and violet, requires white light to be added to it, and as to match the violet with the same blue and red, white light has also to be added to it, it follows that the violet must be freer from white light at all events than the blue.

There is one other experiment that must be mentioned before leaving for a time this part of our subject, viz. the formation of white by a mixture of yellow and blue. If one of the slits be placed in the yellow of the spectrum, a position will be found in the blue where, if a second slit be placed, and the apertures are adjusted, an absolute match with the reflected white of the apparatus can be secured. This experiment will be referred to later on, when considering the question of primary colours.

The above experiments have a great bearing on the theory of colour vision, and should be considered very carefully in connection with the shortened spectrum which we have shown exists when red colour-blind people are observing its luminosity.

There is one point to be recollected in relation to the mixtures of the three or two different colours which make white light. If different coloured pigments be illuminated by the "made" white light, they will not appear of the same hues, as a rule, as when viewed by ordinary white light. They will vary not only in colour, but in brightness. This might be expected when the spectral light which they reflect is taken into account.

CHAPTER X.

Extinction of Colour by White Light—Extinction of White Light by
Colour.

In the last chapter we have shown the impossibility of matching the hue of the simple colours between the violet and the green, unless a certain and appreciable quantity of white light be added to them. We will now turn to a phase of colour measurement which will materially help us to see why, in some cases, the addition of white light to the simple spectrum colours, between the red and green, does not appear necessary in order to make a match with a mixture of red and green.

We will ask ourselves two questions: one is, whether any colour, and if so how much, can be added to white without appearing to the eye? and the other, if any, and if so how much, white light can be added to a colour without its being perceived?

Perhaps one of the readiest methods of explaining exactly what we mean is by a rotating disc. Suppose we have a red disc, of nine or ten inches in diameter, and at every one inch from the centre paste on it a white wafer about one-eighth of an inch in diameter, and cause it to rapidly rotate. On examination we shall find that pink rings will be formed by the combination of the white and red near the centre, but that towards the margins no rings will be visible, owing of course to more red being combined with the same amount of white. This shows that the eye is only sensitive to a certain degree, and cannot distinguish a very small diminution in colour purity. The intensity of the light has something to do with the number of these pink rings which are visible, as may readily be tested in a room. If the rotating disc be placed near a window, and the number of rings visible be counted, a different number will be visible when it is placed in a dark corner. A kindred experiment is to place red circular wafers upon a white disc, and note the rings visible. This gives the sensitiveness of the eye for the diminution in intensity at the other end of the scale. It will be found that there is a marked difference between the two.

It is more instructive if we experiment with pure colours, and so we must resort to our colour patch apparatus described in Fig. 6. If a small circular aperture about quarter of an inch in diameter be cut in a card, and placed in front of the prism nearest the camera lens (Fig. 32), the colour patch, instead of being an image of the face of the prism, will be an image of the circular hole, and when the slit is passed through the spectrum we shall have a coloured spot on the screen, on which we can superpose a patch of white light from the reflected beam. There are two ways in which we can reduce the intensity of the spot, by narrowing the slit through which the spectral ray passes or by placing the rotating sectors in front of the coloured beam. This last, perhaps, is the readiest plan, as it only involves the reading of the sector. We can then diminish the intensity of the coloured spot to such a degree that by its dilution with white light it will entirely disappear. It will be found that red disappears at a different aperture of sector to that required for the green, and the green to that for the blue.

FIG. 32.
Diaphragm in front of Prism.

From our previous experiments in chapter VII. we know the luminosity of the spectrum to the eye, and it will be of interest to see what relation the luminosity at which the spots of different colour disappear, when they are so diluted with white light, bear to the total luminosity of these rays.

In a set of measurements made it was found that the reduced angular apertures required for the colours indicated by the following were:

B	required	300°*	of aperture.
C	required	56°	of aperture.
D	required	14°	of aperture.
E	required	22°	of aperture.
F	required	150°	of aperture.
G	required	2100°*	of aperture.

The large numbers marked with an asterisk were obtained by placing the rotating sectors in front of the white reflected beam.

The light of D had to be reduced to 14° before it was extinguished; therefore to extinguish the original light of this colour in the spectrum would require 180/14, or 12·9 times the intensity of the white light of the reflected beam. With the E light it would take 180/22, or 8·2 times the white light to extinguish it, and so on. If we tabulate the results in this manner, and take the white light necessary to extinguish the D light empirically as 98·5, which is its percentage luminosity in the spectrum of the electric light, we can then compare the extinguishing factor with the luminosity in each case.

Colour.	White required to extinguish the Spectrum.	White required to extinguish the Spectrum, with 50 as that required at E.	Luminosity of Spectrum.
near line B	·6	3·9	4·9
C	3·2	19·5	20·6
D	12·9	78	98·5
E	8·2	50	50
F	1·2	7·5	7·5
G	·087	·56	·6

The very close resemblance between the last two columns indicates that the same luminosity of white light is necessary to extinguish the same luminosity of most colours, within the limits of observation that is to say. Indeed the method of extinction was a plan which Draper and Vierordt essayed, but the results, tabulated from experiments made by them with the apparatus they employed, give a curve of intensity very unlike that given in Chapter VII. In these experiments the luminosity of the orange light corresponding to the D line coming through the slit was measured, and it was found to be 37·5/180 of the white light. Now according to the last table but one 14/180 of this light was extinguished by the full white light, consequently 37·5/180 × 14/180, or 1/62 of the orange light was extinguished by the white light. In other words, if white light be sixty-two times latter when the two are mixed will be invisible. The extinction of all colours requires somewhat more light than this, and a calculation shows that the extinction of every colour is effected by white light, which is seventy-five times brighter than the colour. Artists are well aware that a pale wash of a pigment may be washed over drawing paper, and when dry is invisible to the eye. The above experiments fully account for it.

The other experiment which was to be tried was to see how much white light could be extinguished by a colour. There are several ways by which this can be effected. For instance we may superpose a white dot on the colour patch by placing a card, in which a circular hole is cut, in the reflected beam near the prism, from which the reflection takes place; or by putting a black circular disc of small dimensions pasted on a glass in the same position, by which means the white light is superposed over the whole of the colour patch, with the exception of what, when the colour is cut off, is a black spot; or again by placing a rod to shade half the patch from the white light, but leaving the whole of it exposed to the coloured beam. All these methods have been tried, and it appears that the size of the piece of the patch over which the white light is thrown may have some effect on the resulting curve, but of one thing there is evidence, viz. that a great deal more white light can be mixed unperceived with orange light, than can be with the green, blue, or violet. From one experiment it was found that 1/36 part of white light of the same luminosity as the orange could be mixed with the orange and not be perceived; but that with the green light at E 1/90 would just be visible, whilst at F in the blue-green the 1/120 could be distinguished. Looking at these results, and applying them in elucidating the experiments in which it was attempted, but without success, to match the intermediate colours between violet and green (of which the light at F is a case in point), by mixing them together, unless white light were added to the simple colour; and the success of the other experiment, in which orange light could be obtained of the same hue as that at D by a mixture of the red and green, it will be noticed that 3·3 times more white light can be added to the orange than to the green light at F, without its perception. The white light produced by the mixture in the first case might well show when mixed with the green, but might pass wholly unperceived when mixed with the orange.

CHAPTER XI.

Primary Colours—Molecular Swings—Colour Sensations—Sensations absent in the Colour-blind.

For some purposes it is advantageous to show experiments before indicating the deductions from them which may lead to a theory. Those described in Chapter IX. will enable us to treat the theory of colour perception from a standpoint of some advantage. How is it that the combination of three colours suffices to form white, or to match any colours we wish, be they spectrum colours to which a little white is added, or the colours of pigments? The most plausible theory that can be advanced is that it is only necessary for the eye to be furnished with a three-colour-perceiving apparatus to give the impression of every colour, and yet this would be somewhat difficult to believe had we not had the experiments narrated in that chapter before us. We should have almost expected some machinery in the eye to exist, which would answer to the rhythmic swing of the rays of every wave-length which together make up white light. But now we have to stand face to face with the results of experiment, and we find that at the most only three colours are necessary to make up white light, and that from these three spectrum colours we can form any others, with the limitation already mentioned, when some simple colours are in question.

We must here digress for a moment, and notice the fact that from our experiments we have derived the three primary colours as they are called, viz. red, violet, and green; the definition of a primary colour being that it cannot be formed by the mixture of any other colours. We have ascertained that yellow and blue make white. It is therefore evident that blue, yellow, and red cannot be primary colours, since two of them form white; and we have moreover shown that yellow can be made from green and red; hence it might be fair to assume that the three primary colours are red, green, and blue. But blue, when mixed with a very small percentage of white light, can be made by green and violet. Hence, in the white light formed by the two colours yellow and blue, we have the first made by green and red, and the second by green and violet; hence the three colours which really make the white light are red, green, and violet. The approximate positions of these three colours in the spectrum are those already indicated; though, as we shall presently see, it is highly improbable that any person whose eyes are what are called normal, has ever experienced the fundamental green sensation.

The fact that red, yellow, and blue cannot be primary colours has been mentioned, as even now it is sometimes taught that they are so. As long as the theory of colour principally lay with artists there was reasonable ground for their assumption, since they worked with impure colours, viz. those of pigments; and as we shall see later on the truth of the assumption agreed with such experiments as they would make. When, however, the question was taken up by the physicist with more exact methods of experimenting, and with pure colours, the falsity of the old triad was soon capable of proof.

To return from our digression: how it is that three mixed colours can give the sensation of white light is at first sight hard to understand; but a reference to the action of light on a photographic salt helps us in some degree. In the case of a sensitive salt, such as the bromo-iodide of silver, we find that a chemical decomposition is caused by the violet end of the spectrum, and is only feebly affected by any other part, though with prolonged exposure even the red will cause it. The annexed figure (Fig. 33) gives the idea of the relative action of different parts of this violet portion.

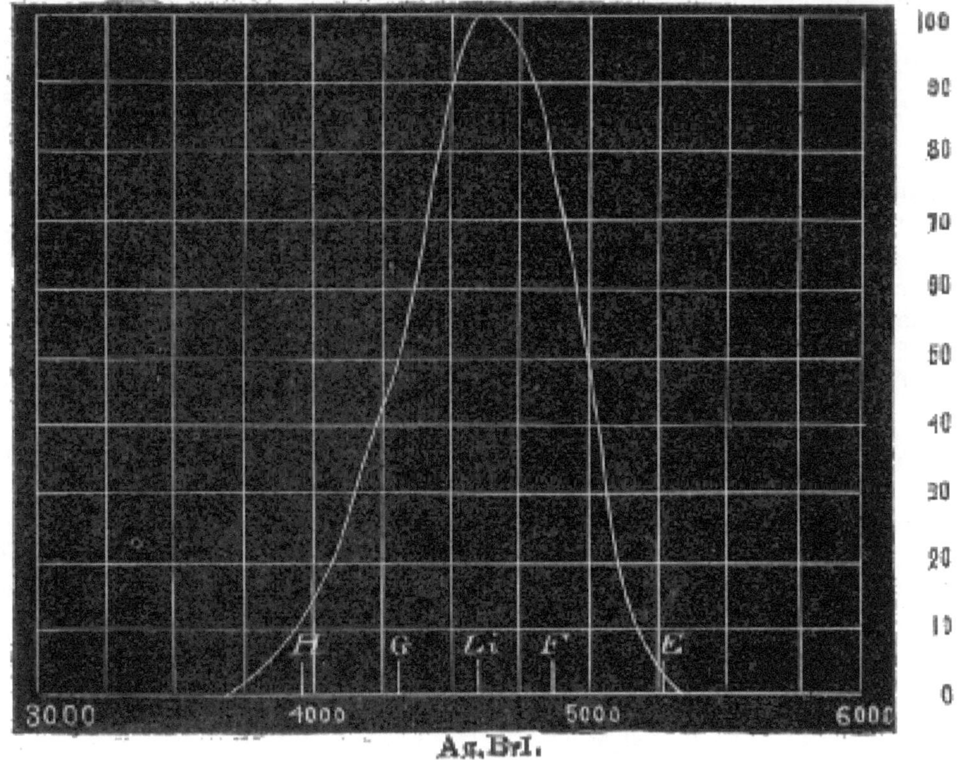

FIG. 33.
Curve of Sensitiveness of Silver Bromo-iodide.

The height of the curve shows the relative effects produced. Now this curve is not symmetrical, but has a maximum effect nearer to the violet end of the spectrum than to the red. The atomic composition of the silver bromo-iodide is probably two atoms of silver and one of bromine and one of iodine oscillating together, and we can conceive of some one atom, the period of whose swings in its molecule is isochronous with some wave-length of light. Further, we can conceive that, like a pendulum whose vibrations are increased in magnitude by well-timed blows, the swing of the atom is also increased, and that eventually it gets beyond the sphere of the attraction of its parent molecule, leaves it, and is attracted to some neighbouring molecule of different constitution, and that thus a chemical change is induced. This we can conceive, but how can other waves, which are not isochronous with the rhythmic swing of the atoms, alter the composition of the molecule? If we have an impulse given to a pendulum exactly timed with the period of oscillation, there is no doubt that the swing is increased. If we have one nearly in accord, it will be found that though the swings are not increased in amplitude so greatly as when there is perfect accord, yet an increased swing is given, and as exact accord is removed further and further, so the increase in the swing of the pendulum gets smaller and smaller. In somewhat the same manner it is possible that many series of waves, differing in wave-length, and therefore in periods of oscillation, may be capable of increasing the amplitude of a swing, and with the photographic salt this probably occurs, with the result which we see in the above figure. Suppose in the eye we have three such sensitive pendulums which are capable of responding to the beats of waves of light, it requires no great imagination to see that one such pendulum will respond not only to that wave of light which is isochronous with it, but also with waves shorter and longer than that particular wave. The same pendulum indeed may respond to the whole of the visible spectrum, but when far off from the maximum the response would be very small indeed. We may therefore assume that though each pendulum may have its maximum increase of oscillation at one part of the spectrum, yet at other parts not only it alone answers to the beating of the waves, but that the other pendulums are also affected by the same, and thus the whole spectrum is recognized by the swings more or less long, of either one, two, or of all three.

To Thomas Young is usually attributed the three-colour theory, though it seems to have been promulgated in an incomplete state some time before; Clark-Maxwell and Helmholtz revived it in later years, and it is usually known as the Young-Helmholtz theory. It should be remarked that the three fundamental colour sensations are not of necessity the same sensations as are given by the three primary colours, as we shall see further on. The following figure (Fig. 34) is taken from Helmholtz's physiological optics, as diagrammatic of the three sensations.

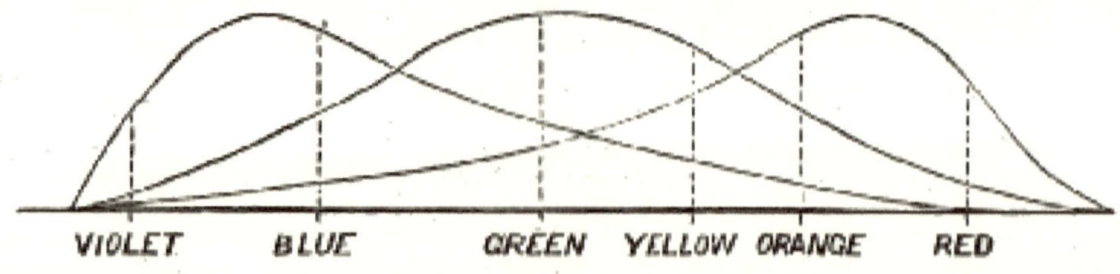

FIG. 34
Curves of Colour Sensations.

To this diagram there is an objection, in one respect, viz. that it gives the same luminosity-value to the blue of the spectrum as it does to the red and green. It has been seen that if we call the luminosity of the yellow 100, that of the blue is about 5. The objection does not hold if it is remembered that the three maxima of impressions are taken as equal. If the ordinates were increased, so that the maxima were of the same height as that of the photographic curve, the resemblance between them and this last would be very marked. It will be noticed that each of the three colour sensations is not only excited by a limited portion of the spectrum, but by all of it, the height of the curves being a measure of their response.

Now assuming that this is the case, since a certain degree of stimulation given simultaneously to the three sensations causes an integral sensation of white light, it follows that the colour perceived in every part of the spectrum is due to the excess of stimulation of either one or two of the fundamental sensations, together with the sensation of white light. If this diagram were correct, at no point in the spectrum is one fundamental sensation excited alone, but we believe that the diagram obtained by Kœnig (Fig. 35), from colour equations (which will be explained in our next chapter), is more exact, and that it is probable that in the extreme violet and extreme red of the spectrum the only sensations which are stimulated are the violet and red respectively. Our measures in the red and violet of the spectrum make it appear that each of the two sensations can be perceived unaccompanied by any others, and the fact that the red colour blind person perceives a shortened spectrum in the red end, is a further proof of this deduction, so far as the red is concerned.

The colour which the fundamental green sensation excites in the normal eye has probably never been seen, nor can be seen. This is due to the fact that all three sensations overlap in the green; that is, that the pendulum which answers to the green colour in the spectrum also affects, but with much less energy, the other two pendulums, which respond to the red and violet sensations.

The word pendulum has been used advisedly, for it may equally as well apply to a molecular aggregation as to one which is visible and measurable. Without entering into the physiological structure of the eye, we may say that it has usually been assumed that the pendulums are the ends of nerves which vibrate with the waves of light; but this seems rather doubtful. Gross matter, such as these ends are, compared with the molecules of which they are built up, cannot, as a rule, vibrate with waves of light, and there seems to be no reason why there should be an exception in the case of the eye. It seems much more probable that a chemical decomposition takes place in some substance attached to them, and where such decomposition takes place electricity of some kind must be produced. In other sensations of the body the nerves act as telegraph wires, carrying messages to the brain, and it is not improbable that the nerves of the eye are employed in somewhat the same manner. Professor Dewar has shown that when light acts on an extirpated eye, a current of electricity does traverse the nerves, and of such an amount that it can be shown to a large audience. This experiment is not, however, conclusive, as the effect may be mistaken for the cause. This idea, however, is only hypothetical, as is indeed the hypothesis of the mechanical action of light on the gross matter of which the rods and cones attached to the retina are composed.

We have in a previous chapter stated that there are some eyes in which the sensation of some colour is altogether absent, and in others in which it is more or less deficient. Thus some eyes appear to be lacking wholly in the sensation of red, others of green, and some very few of violet; and there have been cases known in which two sensations, the red and violet, have been totally absent. In the first case, where the sensation of red is entirely absent, what is known to the normal-eyed as white can be matched with a mixture of blue and green, and there is a place in the spectrum that is recognized as white. Similarly white can be matched by a green blind person with a mixture of red and blue.

To those who may be curious to see the colour which red and green blind persons would call white, a very simple means is at hand to demonstrate it. Using the colour patch apparatus with the three slits inserted in the slide, and in the positions we have indicated in the violet, green, and red, and forming white light for ourselves on the screen, if we cover up the red slit entirely we shall have a patch of sea-green colour, which a red blind person would call white; and if we cover the green slit, uncovering of course the red, we shall have a brilliant purple, which to a green blind person would be white. They both would call white what the normal-eyed person sees as white, for the simple reason that either the red or the green mixed with the remaining colours would be unperceived. The examination of colour-blind people is of prime importance for testing any theory of colour vision. For instance, if it were asserted that the fundamental sensations did not overlap as shown in the diagram above, then it would follow that at some place in the spectrum there would be a dark point. If they do overlap, it must follow that both for the red and for the green colour blind person there must be some place in the spectrum where what is white light to them is produced.

Colour-blind people were tested with the colour apparatus. The reflected beam and the colour patch were made to cast shadows as before, and the rotating sectors placed in the path of the former. A slide with one slit was passed across the spectrum, and the position noted where it was said that the two shadows were illuminated with white light; to the normal-eyed person one shadow of course appeared illuminated with the sea-green colour, or bluish green, according as the observer was red or green colour blind. The ray in the spectrum which to the red colour blind is white, has a wave-length of about 4900, and that for the green colour blind a wave-length of 5020, which corresponds to the position in which we usually place the green slit when a normal-eyed person is making colour matches.

It may be further remarked, that if the maxima of all the three colour sensations are taken, as in the diagram, as of equal value, that the place in the spectrum where the white light is perceived by the colour-blind is where the two sensations are of equal strength, that is, where the two curves cut one another, and are of equal height. By obtaining the proportions of the different colours with colour-blind persons which make up what to them is white light, the curves for the two sensations can be worked out in the form of simple equations.

The experiments carried out with colour-blind people are of the most interesting character, and a good deal remains to be done with the data already obtained from them.

To the popular mind a colour-blind person is usually thought a strange creature, and it is a matter of wonderment, if not of amusement, that they cannot distinguish between the red of cherries and the leaves of the cherry tree. The physicist, studying the theory of colour, views the matter quite differently, and he looks upon an intelligent observer of this class as a boon. It may be remarked that both the red-blind and the green-blind persons would be unable to distinguish between the cherries and the leaves. The red-blind person would see the cherries as green, as also the leaves; whilst the green-blind person would see both as red. Without regarding form it is probable that the red-blind would see the leaves as a bright green, whilst the green-blind would see them as darker red than the cherries. Failure to distinguish between the two is more likely to occur with the green of leaves, and the red of such fruits as cherries, since the former contains a marked proportion of red in it, and the latter a small proportion of green.

One highly-educated gentleman was led to know his deficiency in colour sense, by hearing a companion on a tour going into raptures over a sunset. He saw but little difference between it and that to be seen at midday. Testing his vision it appeared that he was totally blind to the sensation of green, and that white and purple would consequently be mistaken by him for one another. The crimson on the clouds, illuminated by the setting sun, would appear to him as only slightly different to the white clouds which he would see at midday; in fact he would be always seeing what to us would be a sunset. For this gentleman to mix spectrum colours to match others would evidently be no guide to normal-eyed persons.

We believe that amongst us in our daily life we have many persons who are blind to some colour, but who are not aware of it, or if they are aware of it, hide their defect as far as possible. That some are ignorant of it to a late period of their life we know.

We have said that there are cases in which persons are only defective in colour perceptions, and not wanting in them altogether. The former are more common than the latter, and to the experimenter are by no means so interesting. They are only alluded to here to indicate that there are degrees in the defectiveness of eyes to colour. One point which must be remembered here is that all colour production for registration by the mixture of three colours is delusive, unless the eye of the operator is tested for its colour sense.

CHAPTER XII.

Formation of Colour Equations—Kœnig's Curves—Maxwell's Apparatus and Curves.

The plan of obtaining colour equations will by this time have become fairly evident. And we may as well illustrate it by equations obtained with the apparatus we have been using in our previous experiments. Let us suppose we have an individual who is desirous of having his eye-sight for colour tested, and that we have the slide with the three slits *in situ*. It will be found that when we alter their width and form white light with them, matching in purity the white light of the reflected beam, that we shall have to reduce the intensity of the latter very considerably, by means of the rotating sectors. The aperture may sometimes be as small as 4°, and at other times perhaps somewhere between 4° and 5°. Now the variation in aperture between 4°, and say 4·7, is very considerable, but it is highly probable that the latter might be estimated as 4·6, since only degrees are marked on the sectors. It therefore becomes essential to use a less brilliant reflected beam for the comparison, and this is secured by using as a mirror a plain unsilvered glass. What before read 4 will perhaps read 60, and 4·7 will be 70½, whilst 4·6 would be 69, a difference easily read. We can now commence operations. Let us then place the red slit at say (35) of the scale, the green at (28), and the violet at (17), and make white light of the same intensity by altering the apertures of the slits. Let us do the same with the slits at (34), (28), and (17), instead of at (35), (28), and (17); and again make white light, and similarly with the slits at (35), (28), and (18); and let the following be the results—

$$(1)\ 20(35) + 60(28) + 40(17) = 100\ W$$
$$(2)\ 10(34) + 55(28) + 40(17) = 100\ W$$
$$(3)\ 20(35) + 59(28) + 10(18) = 100\ W$$

Subtracting (1) from (2) we get—

$$10(34) = 20(35) + 5(28)$$
$$\text{or } (34) = 2(35) + \tfrac{1}{4}(28)$$

which means that the colour sensation at (34) is made up of two parts of the sensation of (35), together with ¼ part of the sensation of (28).

In the same way we find that the colour sensation of (18) is made up of the sensations of (17) and (28).

$$(18) = 4(17) + 1/10(28).$$

In this way all the different colour sensations can be referred to the sensations which we may happen to consider as best representing the fundamental sensations. What these are is a matter still unsettled; though from the equations formed by colour-blind people, who only require really two colours to form equations, their places are approximately known; evidently as before said, the ray in the spectrum which the green colour-blind person sees as white light, is that where to the normal eye the green fundamental sensation is purest, being free from predominance of either of the other two sensations, and might be taken as a standard colour. Now if our luminosity curve is correct, and if the sum of the luminosities of each colour separately is equal to the luminosity of the colours when mixed (which we have shown to be the case in chapter VII.), it follows that the correctness of the measures can be checked by using the widths of the slits as multipliers of the luminosities. These luminosities can then be added together, and they should equal in luminosity the white light with which the comparison was made. The results can be compared together by reducing the equations to the same standard of white light.

The following is a set of observations which bear this out.

The red and violet slits in this case were kept at 35 and 17·8 on the scale, and the position of the green slit altered.

Position of Slits.			Aperture of Slits.			Luminosity of Colour.			Sum of the Luminosity of Each Colour Multiplied by the Aperture.
R	G	V	R	G	V	R	G	V	
35	28·5	17·8	115	38	112	18·1	73	·65	4930
35	28·0	17·8	119	45	100	18·1	61·5	·65	4989
35	27·75	17·8	122	52	85	18·1	52	·65	4960
35	27·35	17·8	125	65	74	18·1	40	·65	4907
35	27·0	17·8	128	78	67	18·1	33·2	·65	4954
35	26·3	17·8	133	125	40	18·1	20·3	·65	4987
35	26·0	17·8	134	150	10	18·1	16·7	·65	4952
35	25·85	17·8	135	170	0	18·1	15·0	·65	4993
									Mean 4959

The red slit was at a point in the spectrum between C and the red lithium line, and excited probably the fundamental sensation of red alone. The violet slit was close to G, and probably in this case the fundamental sensation of violet was almost excited alone. With the green slit the reverse was the case, all three fundamental sensations being excited. At 26·3 the green sensation was probably the fundamental sensation mixed with white light alone, as at that point the green blind person saw white light in the spectrum, on the red side of it there being what he describes as a warm colour, and on the violet side a cold colour.

An inspection of the table will show how very closely the sum of the luminosities agree amongst themselves, the white light formed by them in each case being of equal intensities. It must be recollected that white light is not necessary to form colour equations; colours may be mixed to form any other colour, which may be taken as a standard. This is often useful in the case of the light between the violet and the blue, where the luminosities are small compared with the luminosity in the green, yellow, and red.

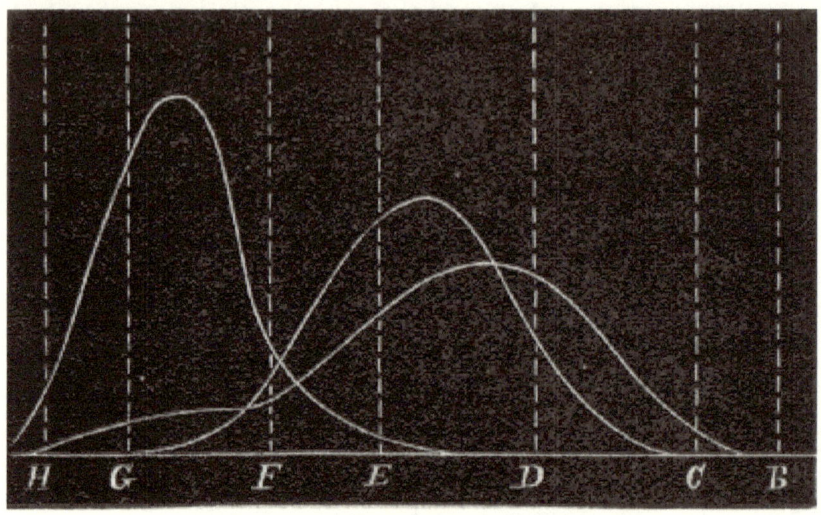

FIG. 35.
Kœnig's Curves of Colour Sensations.

By taking a large number of colour equations, Kœnig, who works in Helmholtz's laboratory, has derived what he considers curves of the three fundamental sensations in a normal-eyed person, and also those of the colour-blind. It may be said that with the colour-blind only two of the fundamental sensations are seen, and therefore only two curves are found, and that these agree in the main with some two of the curves of the three belonging to the normal-eyed.

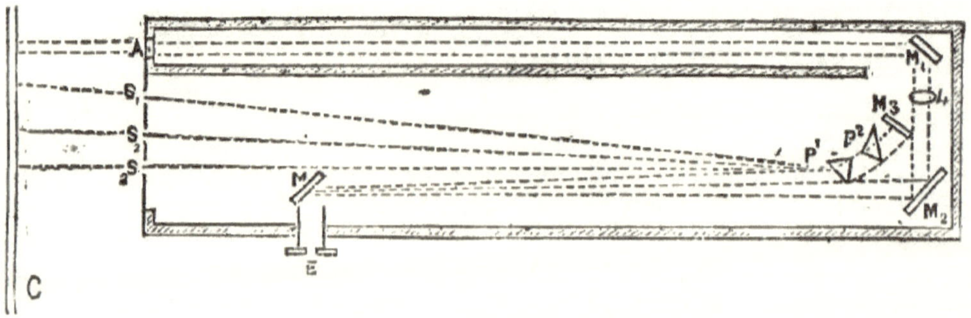

FIG. 36.
Maxwell's Colour-box.

Maxwell was the first to make a definite piece of apparatus for the purpose of obtaining colour equations, and we reproduce from his paper in the *Philosophical Transactions* of the Royal Society for 18—, a somewhat modified diagram of it.

This apparatus is often known as Maxwell's colour-box, and is in fact a spectroscope reversed. With a collimator and prisms we form a spectrum on the focusing-screen of the camera (Fig. 6), by light coming through the slit, and we can obtain light on the distant screen, a patch of any colour, by placing in the spectrum slits as given at Fig. 30. If we were to illuminate the slits so placed with white light, and look through the slit of the collimator, we should see the front surface of the first prism illuminated by the mixture of the colours which would, when the light illuminated the collimator slit, have formed one colour patch on the screen. In Maxwell's apparatus, the slits S_1, S_2, S_3 are illuminated by the light reflected from a white card C, placed in the sunshine, the rays passing through them fall on two prisms P_1, P_2, are reflected back again through these prisms by a concave mirror M_3, are received on another mirror M, and fall at E on to the eye. At A is an aperture in the box, letting through white light on to a mirror M_1, which reflects it through a lens L on to M_2, which again reflects it on to M, and so to the eye at E. Thus at E an image of the prisms, and an image of the aperture are seen, and the white light of the latter can be compared with the mixture of the colours formed by the prism passing through S_1, S_2, and S_3.

Suppose we have one slit S_1, the white light will be decomposed by the prisms, and will be seen at E as light of the same colour as would be seen at S_1, if the light were sent from E to S_1, and so with the other slits. Thus when two or three of the slits are uncovered, the light falling on the eye at E will be a mixture of two or three colours.

There are two drawbacks to the mode of illumination used, one being that the quality of sunlight varies, and therefore colour equations will not be accurately comparable one with the other; and the second is that the light reflected from the card is not absolutely the same in all directions, and it cannot be perpendicularly placed to each of the rays which strike the prisms, after passing through the different slits. This latter is a small objection, and is not of much account, but the first drawback is a more serious one.

With this apparatus, then, Maxwell formed his colour equations, but he fixed as the colours which may be called his standard colours, portions of the spectrum which are certainly not pure, and hence he got curves which are not as perfect as those of Kœnig.

It will be seen, for instance, that his red and violet curves do not overlap, but touch each other near E. Were this true, the green colour-blind person should see a dark space in the spectrum, since the green sensation is missing in such eyes. As a matter of fact the luminosity of the spectrum is very considerable to such a person at this point.

It will also be seen that some of his curves are negative curves lying below the base. This shows that the three standard colours he took are somewhat wrong. The dotted curve gives the combination of his three sensations at every point, and should be the luminosity curve; but owing to his having taken empirically certain standards of luminosity for his three colours, it does not represent the truth, as may be seen on comparison with Fig. 11, page 79.

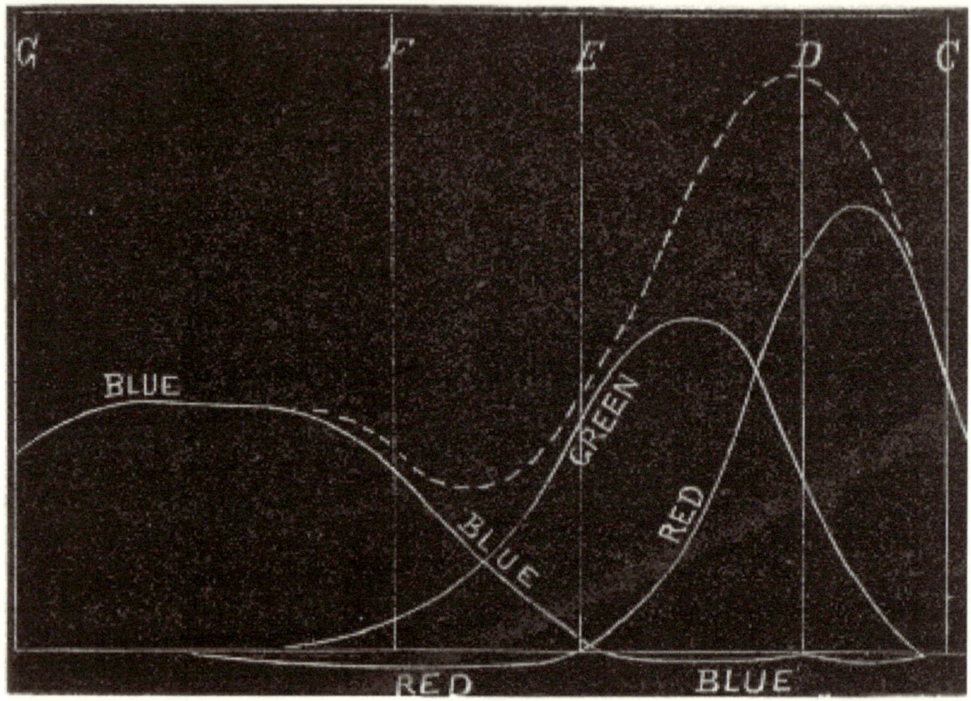

FIG. 37.
Maxwell's Curves of Colour Sensations.

It must be recollected that since Maxwell's observations the subject has been largely experimented upon, and naturally improved appliances and greater knowledge have enabled more nearly correct views to be entertained regarding it.

CHAPTER XIII.

Match of Compound Colours with Simple Colours—All Colours reduced to Numbers—Method of matching a Colour with a Spectrum Colour and White Light.

If we place the solution of bichromate of potassium in front of the slit of the collimator, we shall see that on producing a spectrum on the screen, all rays from the red to the yellow-green pass; hence bichromate of potash transmits a colour which is a compound colour.

It has been shown that this orange colour and the spectral yellow can be matched by mixing the simple colours of red and green together; but it will be instructive to see if a simple colour in the spectrum itself can be found which can match such a compound colour as that of the bichromate.

If we place the bichromate in the reflected beam of the colour patch apparatus and illuminate one shadow cast by the rod with the light transmitted by it, and pass a slit along the spectrum, to produce monochromatic light, with which the other shadow of the rod is illuminated, a position will be found near the orange sodium line "D," where the two colours apparently match in every respect; when the intensities of the two illuminated shadows are equalized as before by the ro-tating sectors. In the same way by filling the part of the square with the pigment on which the shadow illuminated by the reflected beam falls, we can see if we can match emerald green, cyanine blue, and other coloured pigments.

It will often be—more often than not—necessary, however, to dilute the spec-trum colour thrown on the white half of the patch with a trace of white light. By reference to our previous experiments we arrive at what may appear an un-looked-for result, that *no matter what the colour* may be, we can refer it to one ray of the spectrum, together with a percentage of added white light. It is worthy of re-mark, that the place in the spectrum where the simple and the compound colours match, varies according to the kind of light with which the pigment is illuminated. This we can show in a very simple way.

To persons who are totally colour-blind to one sensation, viz. the green or the red, the matching of a compound colour with a simple one in the spectrum should possess no difficulties. Taking the trichromic theory of three sensations for the normal-eyed person, it is evident that only the following classes of sensations are possible in the normal-eyed, the green colour-blind and the red colour-blind—

Normal-eye.   Green colour-blind.   Red colour-blind.

Red	Red	—
Green	—	Green.
Violet	Violet	Violet.
Mixtures of red and green	—	—
Mixtures of red and violet	Mixtures of red and violet	—
Mixtures of green and violet		Mixtures of green and violet.
Mixtures of red, green and violet		—

If we take as a type of colour-blindness the green colour-blind person, we see that every colour in the spectrum must be either pure red or violet, or else these colours mixed with more or less white light, since these two sensations when excited in certain proportions give the sensation of white. At one place, which is commonly called the neutral point, the proportions of the two colours are such that the impression there given is only white; hence it follows that, between this neutral point and each end of the spectrum, the rays are mixtures of violet and white, or red and white, the dilution of the colours varying from no white to all white. As every compound colour must be a mixture of the same two colours in certain proportions, it follows that the green colour-blind person can match every compound colour with some one ray of the spectrum, and that every colour must to him be either red or violet, diluted with different proportions of white light.

In the same way, a person who is colour-blind to the red can also match any colour with a single spectrum colour, and he will see it as` green or violet diluted with more or less white light. This can be readily understood, but it is not quite so plain how any colour sensation felt by the normal eye can be referred to the spectrum.

If we take three rays in the spectrum—one in the red between C and the red Lithium line which we will call R, another in the green between F and b which we will call G, and a third in the violet near G but on the H side of it, and which we may call V—then by varying their intensities (which is equivalent to varying the luminosities) and mixing them, we can give the same impression to the eye that any compound colour gives; and that any intermediate simple spectrum colour gives, if very slightly diluted with white light. With these same three colours, but in different proportions, we can also give the impression of white light to the eye. The intermediate spectrum colours between the green and the violet rays selected when slightly diluted are imitated by mixing these rays together in different proportions, and similarly those lying between the red and the green by mixing together these rays in different proportions—and there is some ray present in the spectrum which, when very slightly diluted with white light, has the same colorific effect on the eye as the mixtures of the pairs v and b, and G and R, in any proportions whatever.

Let the luminosities of the rays R, G and V, which give the impression of white light, be a, b and c units respectively, and p, q and r those which give that of the colour which has to be registered and reproduced. We then get the following equations—where W is white, w its luminosity, Z the colour, and z its luminosity—

$$aR + bG + cV = wW - \text{(i.)};$$
$$pR + qG + rV = zZ - \text{(ii.)};$$

Then evidently—

$$(a + b + c) = w; \text{ and } (p + q + r) = z.$$

Let

$$p = \alpha a, q = \beta b, r = \gamma c,$$

Then we may write (ii.) as—

$$\alpha aR + \beta bG + \gamma cV = zZ - \text{(iii.)}.$$

Now either α, β, or γ must be smaller than the other two. As an example, if α be the smallest, we multiply (i.) by α when we get—

$$\alpha aR + \alpha bG + \alpha cV = \alpha wW - \text{(iv.)}$$

Subtracting (iv.) from (iii.) and we get—

$$(\beta-\alpha)bG + (\gamma-\alpha)cV = zZ - \alpha wW.$$

Now it has already been stated that between V and G there is some ray which gives the same sensation of colour, mixed with a very small quantity of white light, as the above mixture of V and G—let us call it X and its luminosity x [x being evidently equal to $(\beta-\alpha)b + (\gamma-\alpha)c$], and μ the luminosity of the small quantity of white added.

We then get $zZ = xX + (\mu + \alpha)\, W$.

Here we have the colour Z in terms of a single ray, and of white light.

This same holds good when in (ii.) γ is smaller than α and β; but it does not do so should it happen that β is the smallest, for there is no part of the spectrum which contains simple colours giving the same sensation to the eye as mixtures of red and blue. There is, however, a very simple way in which the registration of such a colour (which it must be remarked must be of a purple tone) can be effected. It can be fixed by its complementary. To do this we must add to (ii.) a certain amount of R and V, which will make the whole white. Thus, suppose in (iii.) α to be larger than γ and γ than β, then we must add $\phi bG + \theta cV$ and we have

$$\alpha aR + (\beta + \phi)bG + (\gamma + \theta)cV = nW = Z + \phi bG + \theta cV;$$

but

$$(\beta + \phi), \text{ and } (\gamma + \theta)$$

each equal α $\therefore n = \alpha w$.

$$\therefore Z + \phi bG + \theta cV = \alpha wW.$$

Now between V and G in the spectrum there is some single colour which gives the sensation of the mixture of G and V. Let it be X' with luminosity x', together with white whose luminosity is μ', which must equal $(\phi b + \theta c)$.

$$\therefore Z + x'X' + \mu'W = awW$$
$$Z = (aw - \mu')W - x'X'$$

which again is the colour expressed in terms of white light less the complementary colour. We have thus arrived at the very simple deduction that the hue and luminosity of any colour, however compounded, may be registered by a reference to white light and a single ray of the spectrum.

In practice this dominant ray is very easy to find. Suppose we wish to determine numerically the colour of a signal-green glass in the electric light, we should proceed as follows—

The colour patch apparatus (described in chapter IV.) is employed, and the coloured glass is placed between the silvered mirror which reflects the beam already reflected from the first surface of the first prism of the spectrum apparatus, and the screen, and a square image of that surface of the prism showing the tint of the glass is formed on the screen by means of the lens. Touching this image is a square patch of white light formed by the re-combination of the spectrum by means of another lens. An opaque slide containing an adjustable slit is moved across the spectrum in the manner described in the chapter referred to until the colour of this last patch is approximately the same hue as that of the glass.

In the path of the reflected beam, but between the prism and the silvered mirror, is inserted a piece of plain glass which can be made to reflect part of the beam into the spectrum patch of light, a square patch of the white light being formed by means of a third lens. We thus have monochromatic light mixed with white light. The requisite intensity of the added white light can be adjusted by means of the rotating sectors, as described in the same chapter, which open and close at will during rotation, and the total luminosity of the mixed beams can be altered by this, together with the adjustable slit in the slide. The slit may probably have to be moved in the spectrum to make the hue of these mixed lights the same as that of the glass, but by trial the position of the ray whose colour when diluted with white makes the match is readily found. The position of the slit in the spectrum is noted, as also the aperture of the sectors. The relative luminosities of the beam reflected from the plain glass mirror and of the coloured ray is next measured by placing a rod in the path of the two beams, and equalizing by the sectors the luminosity of the shadows which are illuminated, the one by the spectral ray, and the other by the white light. When the sector aperture is noted the registration is complete, as far as hue is concerned, but the luminosity of the ray transmitted through the glass should be compared with that of the reflected beam, and then the luminosity is also recorded.

Should the colour of a pigment be in question, the ray reflected from the silvered mirror is made to fall on the pigmented surface and the same procedure adopted.

If a purple glass (say) has to be registered, we proceed in a slightly different manner. The patch of coloured light passing through the purple glass is superposed over the spectrum patch, and the slit in the slide is moved till a ray is found which will make white light when superposed on the colour of the glass. The luminosities of this white light, of the reflected beam, and of the spectral colour are compared "inter se," and there are then sufficient data with which to make numerical registration.

Coloured glasses to be used at night with oil or gas, or pigments to be viewed by these lights, must be registered in these lights. As the spectrum colours are always the same, it is convenient to use the electric light spectrum, and the only alteration in the apparatus is to use two gas-lights to illuminate two square apertures, in front of one of which the glass whose colour has to be measured is placed. The images of these apertures are thrown on the screen, the coloured image touching the square image of the spectral colour patch, and the naked image over the latter. The same determinations are gone through as those just described.

The following are the determinations of some glasses—

Glasses Measured.	Wave-lengths of Dominant Ray.	Percentage of White Light.	Percentage of Luminosity of Light Transmitted through the Glass.
Ruby	6220	2	13·1
Canary	5850	26	82·0
Bottle Green	5510	31	10·6
No. 1 Signal Green	4925	32	6·9
No. 2 Signal Green	5100	61	19·4
Cobalt	4675	42	3·75

The following are determinations of some coloured pigments—

Coloured Papers.	Wave-lengths of Dominant Ray.	Percentage of White Light.	Percentage of Luminosity, White Paper being 100.
Vermilion	6100	2·5	14·8
Emerald Green	5220	59·0	22·7
French Ultramarine Blue	4720	61·0	4·4
Brown Paper	5940	50·0	25·0
Brown Paper	5870	67·0	19·5
Orange	5915	4·0	62·5
Chrome Yellow	5835	26·0	77·7
Blue Green	5005	42·5	14·8
Eosin Dye (*Sporting Times*)	6400	72·0	44·7
Cobalt	4820	55·5	14·5

CHAPTER XIV.

Complementary Colours—Complementary Pigment Colours—Measurement of Complementary Colours.

We are now in a position to enter into the question of complementary colours, which is one of supreme interest to artists. A complementary colour, in its strictest sense, may be described as the colour which, combined with the colour whose complement is required, makes up white. In this definition we have three characteristics to take into account, viz. hue and luminosity, and dilution with white light. As an example of what we mean we refer to an experiment which was made and described at page 125. It was said that if the violet slit was placed in a certain position in the blue of the spectrum, it was possible to move the green slit into a part of the yellow, so that the two colours when mixed together would form white. In that case the blue is complementary to the yellow, and the yellow to the blue, so long as the intensities are those which make up white light. Again, if it requires the light coming through the three slits to make up white light, be it the white of the electric light or that of gaslight, we can obtain the complementary colour of the light issuing through any one of them by covering that slit up. Thus suppose the slits to be in the normal position the complementary colour of the red is a green-blue, formed by the mixture of the violet and green rays, the complementary colour of the green is a purple, formed by the mixture of the red and the violet light, whilst the complementary colour of the violet is greenish yellow, formed by the mixture of the red and green rays. It will be evident that as the intensities of the three rays respectively will be different according as the white light matched is the electric light or gaslight, the complementary colours in the former will be different in hue and intensity to those in the latter.

Another couple of striking experiments which the writer devised to show these colours can be made with the colour patch apparatus, and on the same principle as that used for obtaining the intensity of the rays reflected from pigments, and transmitted through coloured transparent bodies. Instead of the small slit with a right-angled prism in front to deflect the beam from the top spectrum, where two spectra are produced (see Fig. 16, p. 95), a single spectrum is used, with a right-angled prism of such a size that it deflects half of it, which is again reflected on to the screen by a mirror, and through a lens to form a second patch of equal size as the undeflected beam. A rod can be so placed in the path of the beams that two coloured stripes are formed, together with a white stripe caused by their overlapping. The two coloured stripes are complementary one to the other. By moving the prism along the spectrum various coloured stripes can be formed, in some cases one being much less luminous than the other, and yet they are complementary. If instead of the large right-angled prism a smaller one be used, the complementary colour due to a small part of the spectrum can be shown in the same manner.

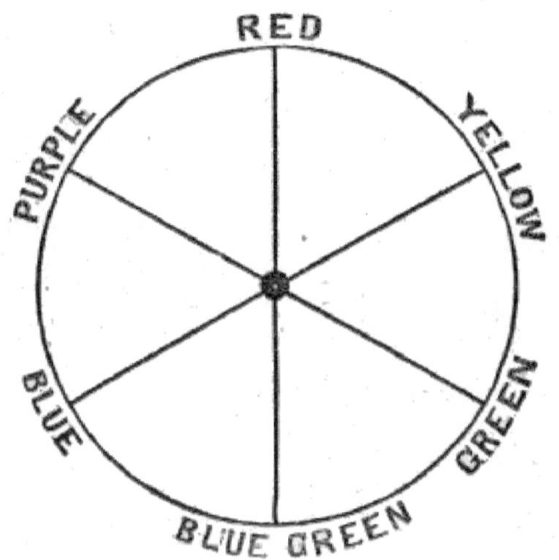

FIG. 38.
Chromatic Circle.

It is customary to show the complementary colours diagrammatically by what is known as the chromatic circle. Roughly it is drawn as in the above figure (Fig. 38). The three colours, red, green and blue, which are taken for primary colours, are placed at 120° apart in a circle, and lines drawn from them through the centre, at which white is supposed to be situated. Where these lines cut the circumference is placed the complementary colour. Other colours can be placed round the circle with their complementary colours opposite, and so a fairly complete diagram of the spectrum can be made. But it must be remembered that this is really of no scientific value, as it conveys no idea of the luminosity of the spectrum colours, nor of the quantities which have to be mixed together to form the complementaries. Such a circle is, however, convenient as a sort of *memoria technica*, and can be filled up according to the fancy of the observer.

The following are pairs of most carefully selected complementary colours of pigments, as adopted by Professor Church.

Complementaries.	Pigments.
Red	Madder red or crimson vermilion.
and	
Green blue	Viridian, the emerald oxide of chromium with a little cobalt.
Orange	Cadmium yellow, of full orange hue.

and	
Greenish blue	Cobalt green.
Orange yellow	Cadmium yellow, or deep chrome.
and	
Turquoise	Cœrulium, or cobalt blue, with a little emerald green.
Yellow	Lemon yellow, pale chrome, or aureolin.
and	
Blue	Ultramarine from lapis-lazuli.
Greenish yellow	Aureolin with a little viridian.
and	
Violet blue	French ultramarine.
Green yellow	Lemon yellow, with some emerald green.
and	
Violet	French ultramarine with madder carmine.
Yellowish green	Lemon yellow with much emerald green.
and	
Purplish violet	Madder carmine with French ultramarine.
Green	Emerald green with lemon yellow.
and	
Purple	Madder carmine with French ultramarine.
Emerald green	Emerald green alone.
and	
Reddish purple	Madder carmine with a little French ultramarine.

As these pairs of pigments are complementary, it follows that if rotated together in proper proportions, they should make a grey which will be indistinguishable from a grey formed by rotating black and white sectors together. (See chap. XV.)

It will probably happen that a good deal more of one of the pairs of the colours is required in the disc than of the other, and supposing that the two are each used of the full brightness which the pigments are capable of giving, it follows that in a diagram where equal areas are filled with the pigments as complementary, some means must be adopted to give the true depth of tone to each. The mixture of white will heighten the luminosity of either, or the admixture of black will lower it, but often alters the hue.

One of the most beautiful methods of observing complementary colours is by means of the polarization of light, which we need not describe in detail. What is known as Brücke's schistoscope is perhaps one of the most convenient. Dove's Iceland spar prism is also useful, when two pigments have to be worked on to paper, so as to be complementary. The two squares of pigmented paper are placed side by side, and two images of each are formed. One image of one colour can be caused to overlap the second of the other, and if the two when superposed appear of a grey they are complementary one to the other. If too much of one colour appears, it must be toned down till the grey is formed. This is a very simple piece of apparatus, and for experiments with pigments will be found to be very handy. When the right tint of each is secured in this manner, a further test may be made by making the pigmented surfaces into sectors, and rotating them together, when if the double-image prism gives correct results, the angular aperture of the sectors should be 180° each, to match a grey produced by a mixture by rotation of black and white.

We have already shown how the complementaries of the spectrum colours can be found; the question is can we find the complementaries of pigments by the spectrum? There is one very self-evident way. We can place the three slits in the spectrum as given in chapter IX., and match in intensity the white light of the reflected beam, and note the apertures of the slits. We must then in the reflected beam place the pigment whose complementary colour is required, and match its colour with the light from the three slits, keeping, for the sake of convenience, the white light falling on the pigmented surface of unaltered intensity, and again note the apertures. If we deduct the last measures from the first, the difference of aperture will give the complementary colour. Thus it was found that with slits in a certain position in the spectrum, to make white light the following apertures in hundredths of a millimétre were required:

$$(1) \begin{cases} \text{Red} & 165 \\ \text{Green} & 60 \\ \text{Violet} & 100 \end{cases}$$

Emerald green was placed in the patch and was matched by the light from the three slits, when it was found that it required

$$(2) \begin{cases} \text{Red} & 4 \\ \text{Green} & 35 \\ \text{Violet} & 25 \end{cases}$$

Deducting one from the other we get as the complementary colour,

$$(3) \begin{cases} \text{Red} & 125 \\ \text{Green} & 25 \\ \text{Violet} & 75 \end{cases}$$

This is a complementary colour, but like the green itself it is mixed with white light; but we can easily deduce what is the simplest complementary colour; for we have only to deduct the possible white light from the second measure. Now evidently the greatest amount of white light is when the whole of the green is taken as forming part of it, with the proper proportions of red and violet, and these we can obtain by taking the proportions of the colours in (1); therefore deduct—

$$(4) \begin{cases} \text{Red} & 69 \\ \text{Green} & 25 \\ \text{Violet} & 41.5 \end{cases}$$

and this would leave as the complementary colour without any admixture of white—

$$(5) \begin{cases} \text{Red} & 56 \\ \text{Violet} & 33.5 \end{cases}$$

which is a purple as would be expected.

Now to give the same dilution of white to the complementary that the emerald green has, we must take away from the emerald green all the white mixed with it, and add that quantity to the complementary. The white in the emerald green can be found by treating the whole of the red as going to form the white; we then have from (1)—

$$(6) \begin{cases} \text{Red} & 40 \\ \text{Green} & 14.4 \\ \text{Violet} & 24 \end{cases}$$

Deducting these from (2), we find that the colour of emerald green, less the white light, is 20·6 of green mixed with 1 of violet. To find the proper dilution of the complementary colour we must add the above proportions of the three colours, and as our final result we find the complementary colour, of equal impurity, is a mixture of—

$$(7) \begin{cases} \text{Red} & 96 \\ \text{Green} & 14.4 \\ \text{Violet} & 57.5 \end{cases}$$

The slits may be set at these apertures and a colour patch thrown on the screen, and we shall find it of a delicate pink. The truth of this can be seen by using a double-image prism to view the pigmented surface, illuminated by the same white light as that in which it was measured, and the colour patch on the screen by its side. The two colours may be caused to overlap, when it will be seen that white is produced.

Another example was an orange pigment, and this we will work out in the form of colour equation. The same mixture gave white, viz.:

$$165\ R + 60\ G + 100\ V = W$$
$$165\ R + 42\ G = O$$

∴ the complementary colour, which is

$$W - O = 18\ G + 100\ V,$$

or a dark-blue colour. In this case there was apparently no white light reflected from the orange. It was slightly glossy, and as polarized light was used for the reflected beam, it was probably somewhat quenched; but what is more probable is that the green contains some violet as well as red, for the reasons given in chapter XI. The reason we have been particular in showing to what extent complementary colours must be diluted with white to the same proportion that the colour itself is diluted, will be apparent if considered for a moment. A deep brown is in reality orange, much degraded in tone, and can be produced as a colour patch on the screen if a bright orange pigment be placed in the reflected beam of the colour patch, and the light nearly shut off by the rotating sectors. Now the same complementary colour will be found for both, but if we were to use the bright complementary colour which we obtained with the orange for the brown, and endeavoured to obtain a white with it by means of the double-image prism we should fail, as the complementary colour would predominate. Complementary colours can always be formed by a mixture of only two rays, and although the overlapping images may form white, yet when the two are placed side by side, it often will be found that the complementary, unless diluted with white, is evidently too dark to be satisfactory, but the luminosity may be increased by adding white to it, as any amount of white may be added to the mixture of the two rays which form the complementary, and of course white will still be formed with the original colour. It is thus quite feasible to give the complementary the same luminosity as the latter by adding white light to it. Like the colour itself, the complementary colour can always be expressed either by a single ray of the spectrum, or by white light from which a single ray is deducted. (See chapter XIII.)

CHAPTER XV.

Persistence of Images on the Retina—The Use of Coloured Discs.

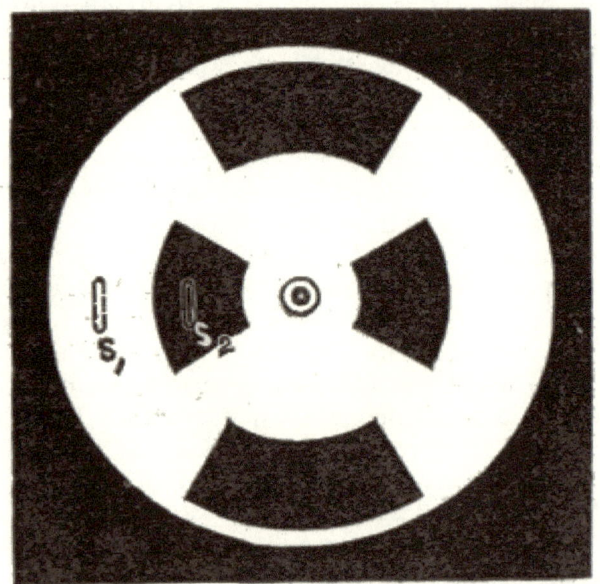

FIG. 39.
Disc to cause alternate opening and closing of two Slits.

By this time we must be thoroughly convinced that by throwing one coloured patch over another a compound colour can be formed; our next business is to demonstrate that the same effect can be produced by successive images of these same colours. Thus we can show that as a mixture of red and blue produces purple, when the two lights are superposed, so precisely the same purple can be produced by allowing the same two colours to strike the eye alternately, and in very rapid succession. We can make a match of the beautiful purple of permanganate of potash as before upon the screen, by placing one adjustable slit in the red and the other in the violet. If we place in front of the slits a disc cut out with equal angular apertures (Fig. 39), the slit S_1 will be covered when the slit S_2 is open, and *vice versâ*, and the two will never be uncovered at the same time when the card is turning round its centre. When this disc is caused to rotate rapidly, we shall have first a patch formed by the light coming through one slit, and then another formed by that coming through the other slit, thrown on the screen on the same place in rapid succession, and the effect on the eye should be precisely the same as if the disc was not there, save in the matter of intensity. Applying this artifice experimentally to the two slits which were used to give the colour of permanganate, the experiment tells us that such is the case. It would be going away from the intention of this work were the physiological aspect of this experiment dwelt upon; it need only be stated that an impression on the retina lasts an appreciable time, though short, and that the impression made by the blue patch has not had time to disappear before there is an impression made by the red patch, and so on. As the retina retains these two impressions together, they produce the impression of purple.

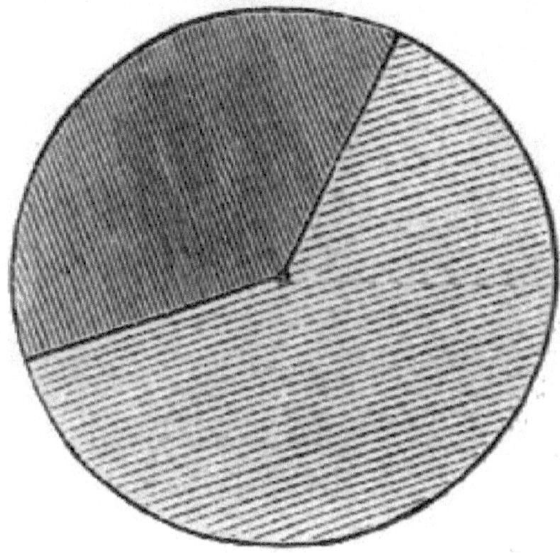

FIG. 40.
Disc painted Blue and Red.

For experiments in colour this duration of impressions is of great value, for we can take advantage of it to compound the colours of pigments together in a very simple manner. For instance, we can take a circular disc painted in sectors with blue and red (Fig. 40), and produce a purple by causing it to rotate round its centre. Small discs of two inches in diameter may be painted with different coloured sectors, and if a pin be passed through the centre, a smart movement of a finger at the periphery will cause it to rotate sufficiently quickly to make the colours blend. A more convenient plan for exact work is, however, to have an electro-motor similar to that which moves the rotating movable sectors (Fig. 41), and at the end of the spindle to fix a cap with a screw and nut attached. The disc, perforated at the centre with a clean-cut hole, can be slipt over the screw, and fastened by the circular nut. When the armature rotates, the disc also rotates at the same speed, and the colours thus blend without any exertion on the part of the observer. Ordinary tops can also be used, but it is somewhat fatiguing to have to wind them up and start them afresh for each experiment. The motor shown in the figure rotates sufficiently rapidly, with discs of eight inches in diameter, to blend colours. It may here be remarked that the stronger the light in which such sectors rotate, the quicker the rotation should be. Too slow a rotation allows a scintillation which is destructive of accuracy of reading. To blend some colours together also requires more rapid rotation than with others. The brighter the colour the more rapid it should be. We learn from this that the diminution of the more intense impressions on the retina is more rapid at first than of the feebler.

FIG. 41.
Electro-motor with Discs attached.

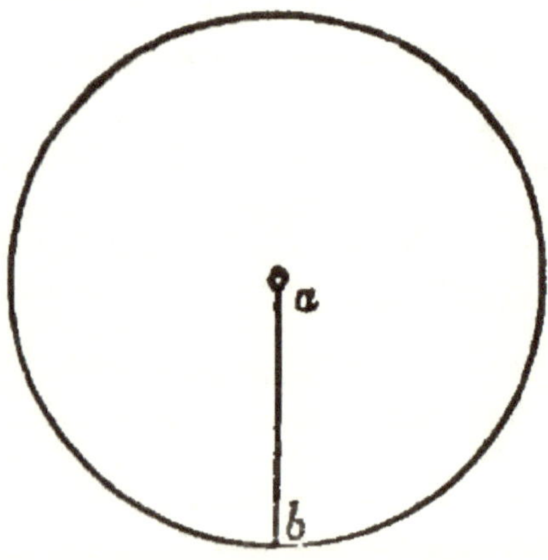

FIG. 42.
Method of cutting Disc to allow an overlap of a second Disc.

Very convenient discs for producing colours by rotation of sectors may be made by the following: vermilion (V), emerald green (E), French ultramarine blue

(U), chrome yellow (Y), lamp-black (X), and (zinc) white (W). With these nearly every colour can be produced, or its value derived. The chrome yellow disc is somewhat superfluous, but is sometimes useful. The alteration in the proportions of the colours can be readily made by Clark-Maxwell's plan. From the circumference to the centre he cut the discs open, as at *ab* (Fig. 42). Any moderate number of discs, similarly cut, may be slipt over one another, and only a sector of each is left visible. It should be remarked that this necessitates the rotating apparatus being viewed with a direct light, as in the case of two or three overlapping discs it is impossible to keep them entirely flat, and shades are apt to be introduced. If we wish to produce a white, or rather a grey, from three colours, we can take three small discs of V, E and U, of equal diameter, and behind them place discs of black and white, of larger diameter, rotating the whole five on a common centre. We shall find that by altering the proportions of the three first we can get a grey which can be exactly matched by a mixture of black and white, X and W. It has already been shown that even lamp-black reflects a certain amount of white light, so this amount of reflected white light has to be added to the white in the outside sectors. In the sectors used in the following experiments it was found that the following proportions of the three colours were required —

$$
\begin{array}{rcl}
V &=& 124° \\
E &=& 143° \\
U &=& \underline{93°} \\
 & & 360°
\end{array}
$$

and to make the same grey it required

$$
\begin{array}{rcl}
X &=& 278° \\
W &=& \underline{82°} \\
 & & 360°
\end{array}
$$

Now the black reflected 3·4% of white light, so that really the proportions of black and white were

$$
\begin{array}{rcl}
X &=& 268·6 \\
W &=& \underline{91·4} \\
 & & 360·0
\end{array}
$$

These matches were made in the light emitted by the crater of the positive pole of the electric light, and are correct only for this light. The greys here are dark greys, and such greys can be matched exactly by throwing the white light in which the comparisons were made on a white card, and reducing the intensity by means of the rotating sectors. We can prove whether our matches are fairly correct from our previous measures of the luminosity of these three colours, in comparison with that of white. The luminosities of V, E, and U, as found from the measures (pp. 93-95), are 36, 30, and 4·4, white being 100; 124 of V would have a luminosity of (124×36)/360, or 12·4; 143 of E would have 11·92; and 93 of U would have 1·14; which, added to either, give a luminosity of 25·46. The luminosity of 91·4/360 of white, which is that of the mixture of black and white, comes to 25·39, so that we may assume our observations have been fairly correct.

The influence of the kind of light in which the match was made is well exemplified by taking the matched discs whilst rotating into a room illuminated by the light from the sky, when it is seen that the grey of the outer discs is bluish; or again, if the matched discs be examined in gaslight, the inner grey will be found too blue.

The match of grey in this last light was found to be

$$
\begin{aligned}
V &= 119° \\
E &= 148° \\
U &= \underline{93°} \\
&\ 360°
\end{aligned}
$$

which matched with

$$
\begin{aligned}
X &= 244° \\
W &= 116°
\end{aligned}
$$

(In this case the black and white are the corrected black and white.)

The importance of making matches in a uniform light is fairly demonstrated by this experiment, and we cannot be wrong in asserting that as skylight and sunlight and cloudlight (the last being often a mixture of the two first), are so variable no measures made on one day can be fairly compared with those made on another, more especially if the observers are different. With an emerald green, a vermilion, an ultramarine, a white, and a black disc any colour may be reproduced in the rotation apparatus, the three first nearly matching what we have already stated to be the three primary colours.

It may seem curious that both black and white may have to be mixed with the colours, to produce a pigment colour; but a little reflection will show how it is. For instance, suppose we want to know the colour composition of gamboge (Y) in terms of vermilion (V), emerald green (E), and ultramarine blue (U). We must make a disc painted with gamboge, and also a black and a white disc of the same diameter, but rather larger than the other three discs, and place them on the spindle of the electro-motor (Fig. 43). We shall soon see on rotating them that no blue is required in the inner disc, and that all that remains to do is to use the red and the green. Mix these two, however, in whatever proportions we may, the mixture will never attain the same luminosity, consequently we must darken the yellow with black. Even then we shall find that, add what black we may, the rotating red and green sectors will always be a little less saturated with colour; which means that on rotation they produce a certain quantity of white light mixed with the yellow. This we might expect, for as emerald green, besides green and red, also contains a fair proportion of blue, and as red, green and blue when mixed give white, it follows that when V and E are rotated together, a grey or subdued white light must be mixed with the colour produced. Turning back to Chapter XIII. we also see that as the emerald green is expressible by a single ray of the spectrum, mixed with white light this result might have been foretold.

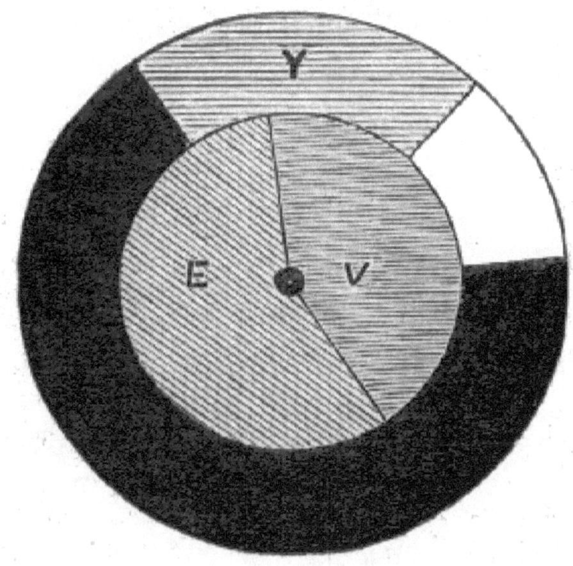

FIG. 43.

**Arrangement to find value of Gamboge in terms of Emerald Green and Vermil-
ion.**

This necessitates adding some white to the rotating sectors of the yellow and black, as the yellow reflects but little white light, and finally we shall get an absolute match, of which the final results are

$$172 \text{ V} + 188 \text{ E} = 75 \text{ Y} + 45 \text{ W} + 240 \text{ X}.$$

This equation is full of meaning. It tells us in the first place what we have already known, that V and E are one or both impure colours, and that when rotated together in the proportions indicated, they produce at least a luminosity of white equal to 53/360 of a white disc (as the black used reflected just 3·4% of white light). Further, it tells us that we can obtain the luminosity of Y, when we know the luminosities of V and E. At page 186, the luminosities of these colours are given as 36 and 30 respectively, white being 100. This makes the luminosity of the colours on the left hand of the equation 17·2 + 15·67, or 32·87, and on the right **75/360** Y + 14·76, and consequently the luminosity of Y = 86·9. In the same way we can obtain any other colour in terms of these standards.

We may here show how we can obtain the luminosity of any colour by means of the three inner discs, and the black and white outer discs. We have already shown that any colour may be matched by the combination of not more than two simple colours, after deducting white from it; and from this we deduce that any coloured pigment will form a grey with some two of the three coloured discs, V, E, and U; and this being done we can then calculate the luminosity. For instance, with an orange-coloured pigment we should proceed to make a disc of the same diameter as that of the three above; an inspection would show us that in this colour red predominates, and therefore we could do without the red disc. We should then alter the proportions of V, U, and O, till they gave a match which was the same as that of a grey given by the rotating black and white sectors.

In an experiment with an orange of this kind, the following results were obtained—

$$\left.\begin{matrix} E & 115° \\ U & 150° \\ O & 95° \end{matrix}\right\} = \left\{\begin{matrix} W & 85° \\ X & 275° \end{matrix}\right.$$

We can now from these deduce the luminosity of the orange employed in this case.

The luminosities of E and U, as already found, were 30 and 4·4, whilst the black (X) reflected 3·4% of white light; we thus get the following equations—

$$115 \times 30 + 150 \times 4·4 + 95\,O = (85 + 3·4 \times 275)\,100.$$
$$\text{This gives } 95\,O = 9435 - (3450 + 660).$$
$$O = 56.$$

That is, the luminosity of the orange is ·56 that of white; by direct measurement it was ·57.

In a similar way the luminosity of chrome yellow (Y) is found. In this case—

$$\left.\begin{matrix} E & 35 \\ U & 204 \\ O & 121 \end{matrix}\right\} = \left\{\begin{matrix} W & 101 \\ X & 259 \end{matrix}\right.$$

Similar equations were formed as the above.

$$35 \times 30 + 204 \times 4·4 + 121\,Y = (101 + 3·4 \times 259)\,100$$
$$\text{whence } Y = 77·6.$$

That is, the luminosity of the chrome yellow is ·78; the same as was obtained by direct measurement.

In the same manner the luminosity of any colour can be found. Thus that of a purple, or of green, can be ascertained; of the former by using the green disc with either the red or the blue disc, and the latter by the red and blue disc. From this it is apparent that we can check the luminosities derived from other means by this plan.

A taking experiment can be made with colour discs to imitate all the colours of the spectrum in their proper order, though diluted more or less by white light. This can be done by rotating V, E, and U together; but in order to get additional luminosity in the yellow, we can use chrome yellow as well. If a disc be made as in the figure (Fig. 44), it will on rotating give a fair imitation of the spectrum, if it be viewed through a slit held in front of the disc.

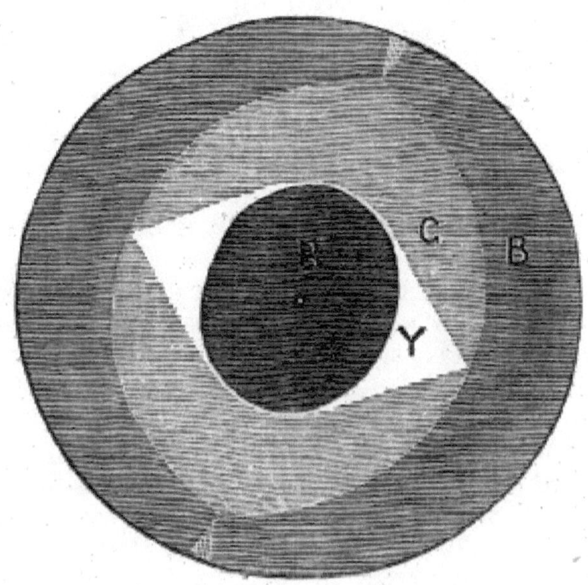

FIG. 44.
Disc arranged to give approximately all the Spectrum Colours.

The mixture of colours by means of rotating sectors is one which the artist cannot use for artistic purposes, and it might seem that for him any deductions made from this method are useless; but it is not so. Suppose we take black lines ruled closely together on paper, and examine the surface from such a distance that the lines are no longer distinguishable it will appear of a grey; and if we take the amount of black on the paper and amount of white, and prepare two sectors of black and white, whose angles are in these proportions, and rotate them alongside the ruled surface, it will be found that the grey of one matches the grey of the other. If instead of lines of black and white we have them of light yellow and cobalt blue, a grey is also produced when the surface covered by the blue is to that covered by the yellow in correct proportions, and may be matched by rotating sectors containing merely black and white. Now some artists employ stippling, filling up cross-hatching of one colour with dots of a totally different colour, or they place dots side by side. When seen from the distance at which the picture should be viewed, these various colours blend one into another, and form a tint which is the same as that which would be obtained by rotating these colours together in the proportion in which they cover the ground. Artists, however, generally mix their pigments together on the palette, and the resulting mixtures are often totally unlike those which are obtained by rotating the same colours together, a noteworthy example is that of yellow and blue. By rotation, and when in proper proportion, these two give a white, but when mixed on the palette a green results. What causes this difference? Experimental proof is always the most satisfactory proof, so let us have recourse to the spectrum apparatus to obtain an answer. Let a spectrum be thrown on the screen, and in it place a strip of paper painted with the yellow, and then another with the blue. With the first it will be seen that the blue rays are not reflected, but only the green and yellow and red, taking the spectrum as roughly made up of these four colours. With the latter the yellow is not reflected, and but very little red, but the blue and the green are reflected strongly. Now we have already said that the reflection of colour from a surface is indicative of the colours the particles of pigments when taken thin enough to be transparent would transmit; hence we may take it that the yellow pigment transmits the red, yellow, and green, and the blue pigment scarcely anything but blue and green. When we have a mixture of these fine particles of pigment on paper, some will underlie the others. But let us pay attention to what would happen if a yellow particle were at the top, and a blue one beneath it. White light would impinge on the yellow particle, but only red, yellow, and green would pass out or be reflected from it. This sifted light would next fall on the blue particle and—as we have seen—only blue and green can pass through or be reflected from it; but as the yellow particle has already deprived the white light of its blue component, the green light alone would pass to the paper, and be reflected either direct from the surface of the paper, or through the particles themselves to the eye. If the blue particle were on the top, precisely the same effect would be produced; it would only allow blue and green to pass to the yellow particle, and as the yellow is opaque to the blue, only green light again would pass. Similarly if side by side the same phenomena would occur, since the light reflected from one on to the other would be deprived of all colour except the green. A very pretty experimental proof of this is to place a yellow solution of dye in front of the slit of the colour apparatus, and having formed the yellow colour patch to place in it a piece of paper covered with a blue pigment: the latter becomes green. By placing a blue solution in front of the slit, and using a piece of yellow pigmented paper, the same result is obtained. The artist therefore in mixing his pigments calls into play the law of absorption, and from his mixtures very naturally assumes that blue and yellow make green. He makes a neutral tint of blue, red, and yellow, and as the red cuts off the green, this naturally follows from the above. Such experiments as these led him to the conclusion that red, yellow, and blue are the three primary colours, an assumption which had he used simple spectrum colours instead of compound colours, such as pigments, he would not have ventured to make.

CHAPTER XVI.

Contrast Colours—Measurement of Contrast Colours—Fatigue of the Eye—After-Images.

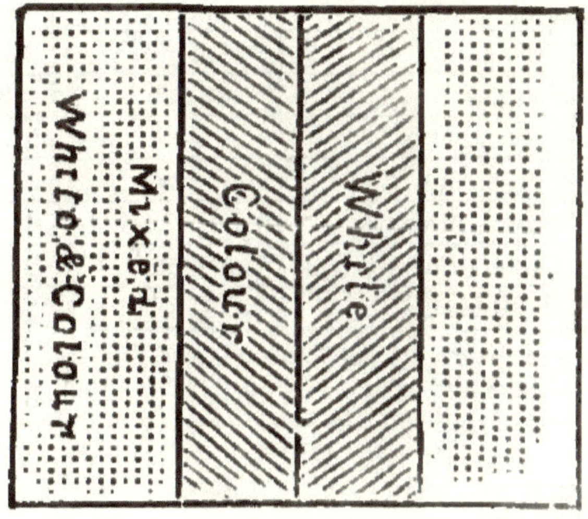

FIG. 45.
Method of showing Contrast Colours.

There is a phenomenon in colour which must be alluded to, and which possesses more than a passing interest to the art world, and that is colour contrast. Perhaps one of the best methods of showing this is by our colour patch apparatus. If we throw the reflected beam and the colour patch on a square as before, and place a rather thinner rod in front, so that the two shadows lie on a background of the combined white light and spectral colours, on passing a slit through the spectrum, the shadow which is illuminated by white light will appear anything but white. Thus if we allow yellow spectral light to illuminate one shadow, the other will appear decidedly of a blue hue; if a green ray it will be of a ruddy hue; if a blue ray of a yellow hue; that is, all the contrast hues will appear to the eye to tend towards a complementary tone to the spectral light. The kind of white light illuminating the shadow has a marked effect on the tone, as might be expected. The following table shows the contrast colour of the white illuminated shadow when the white light used was that of a candle.

Spectrum Colour.	Contrast Colours in Electric light.	Spectrum Colour.	Contrast Colours in Gaslight.
Cherry red	Green gray	Cherry red	Green gray
Scarlet	Bluish green gray	Scarlet	Sap green
Terra-cotta	Blue gray	Light red	Green gray
Raw sienna	Light blue gray	Olive green	Pink gray
Olive green	Umber	Apple green	Mauve & black
Emerald green	Pinkish lavender	Emerald green	Pink terra-cotta
Grass green	Light pink	Emerald green	Pink terra-cotta
Bluish green	Dark pink	Bluish green	Pinker terra-cotta
Signal green	Salmon	Peacock blue	Salmon
Cyanine blue	Yellow ochre	Prussian blue	Reddish yellow
Ultramarine	Raw sienna	Ultramarine	Raw sienna
Violet blue	Brownish yellow	Violet blue	Brownish orange
Blue violet	Green yellow brown	Blue violet	Brownish yellow
Violet	Burnt sienna	Violet	Yellow ochre

The contrasts here shown are not so visible when the two shadows of the rod occupy the whole of the white square, but are decidedly increased by the shadows occupying only a part of the field, the margins being illuminated with a mixture of the two lights. Not only are there contrasts with coloured light and white, but the relative position of one colour to another may alter the hue of each to the eye. The following experiments indicate what change can be expected in contrasted colours. The double colour apparatus was used as described at page 122, and a slit was placed in four different positions in the spectrum, viz. in the red, orange, green, and violet, to form patches, and another slit was placed in the same four positions in the other spectrum, and the contrasts noted.

Original Colours.		Change due to Contrast.	
Red	Orange	Red became yellower	Orange became green grey
Red	Green	Red unaltered, but brighter	Green unaltered, but brighter
Red	Blue	Red became more orange	Blue became greener
Red	Violet	Red became orange	Violet, no marked change
Green	Orange	Green became bluer	Orange became yellower
Green	Blue	Green became olive	Blue became more violet
Green	Violet	Green became yellower	Violet became bluer
Orange	Blue	Orange became redder	Blue became bluer
Orange	Violet	Orange became greener	Violet became bluer

| Violet | Blue | Hardly altered | Hardly altered |

These contrasts were in most cases very marked, as would be seen by causing the same colours to fall on a different part of the screen, outside that on which the comparisons were made.

This phenomenon of contrast is one which is most valuable for artistic purposes, for it gives a power of increasing the value of the colour of pigments which is used by the artist almost intuitively. Thus he can heighten the tone of his orange pigment, with which he makes a sunset sky, by placing in juxtaposition with it some bit of blue coloured space. The blue becomes bluer, and the orange more orange, by this artifice. All these artifices—or rather we should say intuitive applications of science—are most necessary when the small range of luminosity of colours with which he has to deal is taken into account. For instance, in a picture of a sun-lighted snow mountain and deep pine forests, the utmost luminosity he can give to the former is that of white paper when seen in the shade, which, in comparison with what he sees, is really a mixture of 90% of black with the light from the snow, so that his range of luminosity is only nine-tenths of that which occurs in nature. It is in adapting this low scale to his picture that true genius of the artist is seen.

It might seem that these contrast colours being only a physiological effect, could not be accurately measured, but such is not the case, if a little artifice be employed. If we use the second colour patch apparatus side by side with the first, we can very readily and with very close approximation determine the contrast colours we see. Suppose by the second apparatus we form a colour patch of say red, and place a thin rod in the beam of this ray and of the reflected beam, and about six inches from it form another patch with the first apparatus, using the three slits to make colour mixtures; by first noting the contrast colour, and then approximating in the second patch to what the eye perceives, we can little by little get a fairly exact match to the contrast colour, and can definitely note it. We now give the results of three measures made for the contrast colours which presented themselves to the eye when they were caused by a red ray near the lithium line, another near the E line in the green, and the third near the G line in the violet.

To make white light and the contrast colours, the slits had to be of the following apertures—

COLOUR.	RED.	GREEN.	VIOLET.
White light	15·7	6·5	9·8
Contrast to Red	13·5	11·8	22·5
Contrast to Green	15·8	5·1	4·8
Contrast to Violet	15·9	7·2	4·2

Thus to form the contrast to red took 13·5 of red, 11·8 of green, and 22·5 of violet. Now from each of these there can be deducted the amount of white light, which will leave only two colours mixed. Calculating this out we find that the contrasts are—

Contrast Colour to	Red.	Green.	Violet.
Red	—	3·5	16·7
Green	15·7	3·2	—
Violet	19·4	9·5	—

If the contrasts were exactly complementary colours, the proportions of the two colours left should be the same as those of the same colours as given, which with the original colour make white light. It will be seen that such is not the case. A very simple way of testing this is to form a patch of white light with the three slits in the first apparatus, and then to obtain the contrasts by the other apparatus, with the same colours one after the other that pass through the three slits. If now we cover up the slit in the first apparatus through which the colour whose contrast in the second apparatus is sought passes, we may dilute it with white light as we will, but in no case has the writer found that an exact match to the contrast colour can be obtained in this way. Thus, supposing we wanted to try the experiment with the same red light as that which comes through the red slit, we should use that same light in the second apparatus, and form the contrast colour with the white beam, and then in the first apparatus cover up the red slit, leaving the violet and green to form a patch on the screen. We should then dilute the colour of this patch with white light, and note if it appeared the same as the contrast colour.

Another phenomenon which presents itself is the fatigue of the colour-sensation apparatus of the eye, induced by looking at a bright object. For instance, if we look at a crimson wafer or spot for some time, and then turn the eye so that it rests on a grey surface, an image of the spot will still be seen, but as of a greenish-blue colour. This is due to the fact that the red-seeing apparatus is fatigued and exhausted, whilst the green and violet-seeing machinery has not been largely exercised. Consequently when looking at grey paper the grey of the paper is seen in the retina at all parts as grey, except in the small part of the retina which has got diminished power of perceiving a red sensation; hence a sea-green image will be seen until the fatigue has passed away. This colour can be reproduced with very fair accuracy by allowing only one eye to be fatigued, and then using the other to obtain a colour mixture corresponding to it. It will then be found that the colour is the same as the complementary colour, much diluted with white light.

To the same cause may be traced positive and negative after-images, as they are called. If we look at a strongly-illuminated coloured form, such as a church window, and close the eyes, the window will still be seen, at first of its original colour (a positive after-image), and it will then fade and be seen in its complementary colours (a negative after-image). The positive image is due to the persistence of what we may call nerve irritation, whilst the negative image is due to the physiological excitation of all the nerve fibrils, which ordinarily speaking give the sensation of a very dull white light. The previous fatigue of one set of fibrils, however, prevents them being excited to the same degree as the others, hence we get a complementary image. It would be out of place to pursue this subject further, as we have only dealt with the physical measurement of colour-sensations, and these are beyond it.

INDEX.

A

After Images *1*

B

Balmain's Paint *12*
Black Body *4*
Bromo-Iodide Of Silver *69*

C

Carbon Poles *5*
Colour Equations *71, 74, 76, 77*
Contrast Colours In Electric Light *100*

E

Extinction Of White Light *64*

F

Fluorescence *11, 12*
Fundamental Sensations *71, 72, 75, 76*

G

Glass Prisms *6*
Glow-Worm *1, 2*

H

Hue *2, 3, 10, 22, 26, 30, 40, 45, 59, 62, 64, 67, 82, 84, 85, 87, 99, 100*

I

Impression Of White Light *37, 80*
Infra-Red Rays *12*

L

Luminosity Of Chrome Yellow *96*

M

Mock Sun *26, 27*

P

Particles Of Water *26, 30*

R

Ritter's Rays *12*
Rotating Sectors *16, 18, 19, 32, 36, 55, 56, 58, 59, 62, 64, 65, 72, 74, 79, 82, 89, 93, 95, 97*

S

Simple Colours *3, 4, 21, 22, 57, 61, 64, 68, 79, 81, 95*
Soap-Bubbles *24*
Spectrum Of Sunlight *4, 8*
Sunset Clouds *26*
Sunset Sky *101*

U

Ultra-Violet Rays *11, 12*

W

White Light *3, 6, 17, 18, 19, 21, 23, 24, 26, 32, 34, 37, 40, 48, 49, 52, 53, 54, 57, 58, 60, 61, 62, 63, 64, 65, 66, 67, 68, 69, 71, 72, 74, 75, 76, 77, 79, 80, 81, 82, 83, 84, 87, 88, 89, 90, 93, 94, 95, 96, 98, 99, 100, 101, 102*

Y

Yellow And Blue Make White *68*
Yellow Spot *59, 60*
Yellow Spot *57*
Young-Helmholtz Theory *70*

Lector House believes that a society develops through a two-fold approach of continuous learning and adaptation, which is derived from the study of classic literary works spread across the historic timeline of literature records. Therefore, we aim at reviving, repairing and redeveloping all those inaccessible or damaged but historically as well as culturally important literature across subjects so that the future generations may have an opportunity to study and learn from past works to embark upon a journey of creating a better future.

This book is a result of an effort made by Lector House towards making a contribution to the preservation and repair of original ancient works which might hold historical significance to the approach of continuous learning across subjects.

HAPPY READING & LEARNING!

LECTOR HOUSE LLP
E-MAIL: lectorpublishing@gmail.com